The Protestant Wedding Sourcebook

A Complete Guide for Developing Your Own Service

SIDNEY F. BATTS

Westminster/John Knox Press
Louisville, Kentucky

To Cathy, Meredith, and Emily . . .
the treasures of my life

Book design by ediType

First edition

This book is printed on recycled acid-free paper that meets the
American National Standards Institute Z39.48 standard.

Published by Westminster/John Knox Press
Louisville, Kentucky

PRINTED IN THE UNITED STATES OF AMERICA
9   8   7   6   5   4

Library of Congress Cataloging-in-Publication Data

Batts, Sidney F.
    The Protestant wedding sourcebook : a complete guide for
developing your own service / Sidney F. Batts. — 1st ed.
        p.   cm.
    ISBN 0-664-25303-2 (pbk. : alk. paper)

    1. Marriage service. I. Title.
BV835.B348 1993
265′.5—dc20   92-19807

Contents

PART I

Designing Your Own Wedding

PART II

Wedding Services from Protestant Churches

PART III
Additional Helps

Acknowledgments

This book is the product of many years of working with engaged couples who took this work, in its many forms, and used it to design their own wedding services. Continual revision has been the result of their input and observations. A special thanks goes to the engaged couples of the Presbyterian Church of Lowell, North Carolina; to the engaged couples of the Mount Vernon Presbyterian Church of Atlanta; and in particular to those of the First Presbyterian Church of Dunn, North Carolina. During the past thirteen years these men and women have contributed much to my insight. Most of all, they seemed thrilled to have the opportunity to design their own service, which gave me inspiration that such a book would be a welcome resource for other engaged couples.

Constant companions in this book's journey have been my secretaries, Evelynn Cameron and Margaret Lee. They faithfully assisted me and the engaged couples by typing the designed wedding services. Additionally, they offered helpful insights along the way as this book evolved.

Several others assisted me along the way. Reverend Joey Hester, who was then in the seminary, gave me a seminary student's perspective and offered helpful suggestions. Colleagues and special friends, John R. Wall, Jim Bumgardner, and Emily Duncan Rosencrans, encouraged me that such a book was a needed resource for clergy. Parishioner Dr. Walt Walker patiently assisted me with his computer and word processing skills, and good friends and former parishioners Bob and Janet Bryan facilitated this book's development by generously providing me with several weeks at their coastal cottage.

Lastly, I owe much to Walt Sutton and his colleagues at Westminster/John Knox Press who thought this work worthy of publication.

Grateful acknowledgment is made to reprint or adapt the following copyrighted material.

Church of Scotland
The First Order for the Celebration of Marriage from *The Book of Common Order (1979),* Church of Scotland, is used by permission of the Rev. Charles Robertson, Manse of the Canongate, Edinburgh. (P. 92)

Church of South India
The Marriage Service from the Church of South India is reprinted from *The Church of South India Book of Common Worship,* by permission of Oxford University Press. Excerpts from the Book of Common Prayer of 1662, the rights in which are vested in the Crown in perpetuity within the United Kingdom, are reproduced by permission of the Crown's patentee, Cambridge University Press. (P. 95)

Evangelical Covenant Church of America
The Rite of Marriage II from *The Covenant Book of Worship* is copyright © 1981 by Covenant Publications, Chicago, Illinois. Used by permission. (P. 107)

Lutheran (1958)
The Order for Marriage is reprinted from SERVICE BOOK AND HYMNAL, copyright © 1958, by permission of Augsburg Fortress. (P. 110)

Lutheran (1978)
The Marriage Service is reprinted from LUTHERAN BOOK OF WORSHIP, copyright © 1978, by permission of Augsburg Fortress. (P. 113)

Methodist (1964)
"The Order for the Service of Marriage" is reprinted from *The Book of Worship of the United Methodist Church,* copyright 1964, 1965 Board of Publication of The Methodist Church, Inc. Reprinted by permission. (P. 116)

Methodist (1985)
"A Service of Christian Marriage" is reprinted from *The Book of Services,* copyright © 1985 The United Methodist Publishing House. Reprinted by permission. (P. 119)

Moravian
"Solemnization of Matrimony" is reprinted from *Hymnal and Liturgies of the Moravian Church,* 1969, and is used by permission. (P. 124)

Presbyterian (1946)
"The Order for the Solemnization of Marriage" is reprinted from *The Book of Common Worship,* copyright 1946 The Board of Christian Education of the Presbyterian Church in the United States of America. Used by permission. (P. 126)

Presbyterian (1970)
"The Marriage Service" is reprinted from *The Worshipbook: Services and Hymns.* Copyright © MCMLXX, MCMLXXII The Westminster Press. Used by permission of Westminster/John Knox Press. (P. 129)

Presbyterian (1986)
"Christian Marriage: A Service for General Use" (Rite I) is reprinted from *Christian Marriage* (Supplemental Liturgical Resource 3). Copyright © 1986 The Westminster Press. Used by permission of Westminster/John Knox Press. (P. 131)

Reformed Church in America (1968)
The "Order of Service for the Solemnization of Marriage" is reprinted from *The Liturgy of the Reformed Church in America, Together with the Psalter,* and is used by permission. (Pp. 137, 140)

Reformed Church in America (1987)
The "Order of Worship for Christian Marriage" is reprinted from *Worship the Lord* (Grandville, Mich.: Reformed Church Press), and is used by permission.

United Church of Canada (1950)
"An Order for the Solemnization of Matrimony" is reprinted from the *Book of Common Order of the United Church of Canada* (1950) and is used by permission of the United Church Publishing House, United Church of Canada, Toronto. (P. 144)

United Church of Canada (1985, Rites I and II)
The "Celebration of Marriage" Wedding Services from the United Church of Canada are used by permission of the United Church of Canada. (Pp. 146, 152)

United Church of Christ (1969)
"The Order for Marriage" is reprinted from *Services of the Church* (New York: United Church Press, 1969), and is used by permission. (P. 155)

United Church of Christ (1986)
The United Church of Christ Order of Marriage is used and adapted by permission from the *Book of Worship, United Church of Christ,* © 1986 United Church of Christ, Office for Church Life and Leadership, New York, New York. (P. 158)

Uniting Church in Australia
The Marriage Service is from *Uniting in Worship Leader's Book,* copyright © 1988, The Uniting Church in Australia Assembly Commission on Liturgy. Used by permission of the Joint Board of Christian Education, Melbourne, Australia. The Acclamations from *The Alternative Service Book 1980,* copyright © The Central Board of the Church of England, are used by permission. Excerpts from the English translation of *Rite of Marriage* are copyright © 1969, International Committee on English in the Liturgy, Inc. All rights reserved. Used and adapted by permission. The Great Prayer of Thanksgiving is used by permission of The United Church of Canada. Other prayer selections are used by permission of Westminster/John Knox Press. (P. 166)

To the Minister

I had not been in the ministry a month before I had two weddings on my calendar. When I searched for my denomination's wedding services, I found one that was traditional in form but archaic in language and another that was contemporary in language but untraditional in form. One of the engaged couples wanted my help in merging the contemporary language into the traditional form.

I soon began my journey to find wedding services in the mainline Protestant traditions that spoke to couples and the Christian community as we gathered to worship God and celebrate marriage. What I found among the various Protestant services was a similarity within mainline Protestantism. This was especially true in the form of the service. Yet I was also surprised to find that the content of Protestant wedding services contained subtle but sometimes profound differences. I began to share these different services with engaged couples. I gave instructions for them to read and compare the different services and to pick and choose the sections they liked. When the couples returned, we tried to piece the services together to form *their* wedding service. Over the years, and as I shared a variety of wedding services, the couples began to mix and match with greater frequency.

Several years ago I had a simple idea. I had come to realize that the basic Protestant wedding service has eleven general sections. Therefore, I took the Protestant wedding service and divided it into categories. I organized these categories into a notebook and asked the couples to choose a selection from each category. The result was a "created," or at least edited, wedding service. The couples loved the idea!

It gave them the opportunity to shape their own service. Plus, it gave them a firsthand look at what was said in the wedding service — indeed, in their wedding service. One of the immediate payoffs of the notebook was that it gave the couple a serious review of their intentions, vows, and commitments. From the perspective of a premarital counselor, the wedding notebook provided a valuable instrument for the engaged couple. They were forced to deal with their own hopes, intentions, and expectations as they jointly read the vows, the statements on marriage, and the other contents of the wedding service.

Since the early days of the wedding notebook, I have added many more selections from various Protestant churches. I have also included in this sourcebook the original and unedited wedding services from various Protestant traditions. In the past decade, several denominations have produced excellent wedding services. I regret, however, that I have been unable to provide services from autonomous traditions such as the Baptist, Congregational, and Disciples of Christ churches. There are no official wedding services representing these traditions.

There may be objections to a sourcebook like this. Some may wonder how a wedding service that is part Methodist, part Lutheran, and part Presbyterian can possibly hang together theologically or stylistically. But I think you will find, as I have, that there is little theological and stylistic difference. Generally speaking, the Protestant services are the same in theological emphasis and form, with subtle stylistic differences but with occasional profound distinctions in content.

9

The major problem confronting this sourcebook is the diversity of language used in the wedding services. Most of the older services use archaic words such as "thee," "thou," "keepest," or "troth." Indeed, it would be awkward to have a combined service that uses archaic English sometimes and contemporary language at other times. Therefore, I have tried to remove most of the archaic language in the selections so that today's vernacular is present. "Troth" has been replaced with "faithfulness," and so on. Also, I have tried to use inclusive language where possible, substituting "humankind" for "mankind," "men and women" for "men," and so on. However, the section of this sourcebook that includes the original wedding services from various denominations (part 2) is unedited. These services have been left unaltered and stand in their original form and language. Of course, these services may be the very ones the couples select. In any case, they stand as a valuable resource for any minister.

As the minister, you are the final editor. I suggest that you sit with the engaged couple after they have completed the enclosed worksheet and suggest alternatives if needed. Occasionally the couple is undecided about a selection, or in need of advice about a particular area of the wedding service. One such area might be Category 5 — "Leavetaking." This sourcebook gives alternatives that differ from the traditional "giving away" of the bride. The couple may want to consider involving both families and/or the congregation at this point in their wedding service. One of the options in this sourcebook is to design a wedding service that stays primarily within a certain tradition, save for a few changes in a category or two. Or, if you have a Lutheran marrying a Methodist, then it is entirely possible to have a service that combines both traditions. Endnotes will indicate the denominational tradition of each selection. The advantage of this wedding sourcebook is the flexibility it provides for both minister and couple.

To the Engaged Couple

Congratulations on your forthcoming marriage! This sourcebook is designed to give you options and input for your wedding service. The book is also designed to make you aware of variations among Protestant wedding services, assist you in thinking through your service, and give you the opportunity to choose, edit, and design a service that will be meaningful for you. You also have the option to use an already existing service that is the product either of your church tradition or of another Protestant church tradition.

The advantage of this book is that it allows you the flexibility of designing a wedding service that is uniquely yours. Yet it does that without placing upon you the unrealistic burden of writing your own vows or other parts of the wedding service. Indeed, as you read through this book and fill out the "Wedding Sourcebook Worksheet" (see pp. 19–20) you will have designed a wedding service that is traditional in nature, both in form and in language. Most of the selections you will be examining will be portions, or slight variations, of existing wedding services within mainline Protestant churches. Each selection, however, will speak to you because you, as a couple, have selected it, thought through it, listened to how it sounds, and decided what it means to you. It will be *your* service; and yet, at the same time, it will be a time-honored service of the church.

On the page entitled "Traditional Wedding Service Order" (see p. 18) you will see the traditional order for the Protestant wedding service. If you compare wedding services from the various traditions, whether it be Presbyterian, Methodist, Episcopal, or another, you will find that there is little difference in the order of the services. One service may include a prayer where another does not. One service may not have a charge to the couple; another one may include a scripture lesson. However, generally speaking the variations of Protestant wedding services are slight.

Perhaps the most troubling aspect for today's engaged couple is when you desire a traditional service, but the language is so archaic that it loses its meaning for you and for the gathered congregation. Most of us do not say "ye" or "thou" or "thy" or "wilt" in our conversations. Nor do we employ archaic English and use sentences with "keepest" or "goest." Nor do we use or understand terms like "troth" or "infirmities." Yet all of these are included in the traditional wedding services. In order to help you avoid this linguistic dilemma, the selections in the eleven categories given in part 1 have been edited so that they use contemporary, up-to-date language. Therefore, if you use this sourcebook to design your own wedding, you will avoid having to use outmoded language. In the selections in part 1 care has been taken to remove the "thees" and "thous" and the other words and phrases that have lost their meaning in today's language. They have been replaced with "he" and "you," and words like "troth" have been replaced with "faithfulness." Also, this sourcebook has tried to use inclusive language so that, for instance, instead of "men," synonyms are used such as "men and women" or "people"; or, instead of "mankind," "humanity" or "humankind" is used.

11

However, you may decide to use one of the already existing wedding services that are printed in this book in part 2. These services come from various church denominations and can be used as is. Whether you decide to design your own service by using the "Wedding Sourcebook Worksheet," or use one of the existing denominational services, it is wise to read and study the wedding service from your own church denomination. Your minister will gladly assist you if you have questions or concerns about your wedding service.

You will find this sourcebook an invaluable tool as the two of you are led to think through the vows, commitment, expectations, and responsibilities of your marriage. You will be led to take a thorough look at what you will be saying and hearing on your wedding day. The "Instruction Page" (p. 17) will give you directions to design a meaningful wedding service. In part 1 you will find a section entitled "Helpful Insights in Examining the Selections" (pp. 21–22). That section examines issues in some key categories and may guide you in choosing one selection over another.

Have fun . . . and may this wedding sourcebook set you on your way to a meaningful wedding service and a joyous marriage.

To the Church Secretary

Typing the wedding service for the engaged couple is an important step in the preparation for the wedding. Your help is essential for things to run smoothly on the wedding day.

When the engaged couple or the minister brings *The Protestant Wedding Sourcebook* to you, along with the completed "Wedding Sourcebook Worksheet," you will be almost ready to begin. But before you begin, take a look at this entire book in order to familiarize yourself with its contents. You will be dealing primarily with part 1, "Designing Your Own Wedding." First, read carefully the sections entitled "To the Engaged Couple" (pp. 11–12), "Instruction Page" (p. 17), and the "Wedding Sourcebook Worksheet" (pp. 19–20). When you have completed those, turn to the back of the book and review the sample worksheets and the sample wedding services that are the result of those worksheets. Consult with the minister about his or her preferences on how the service is to be typed. My secretary types each wedding service on folded, legal size paper and then photocopies it on to a heavy bulletin-stock paper. This is easily folded and ready to use at the time of the wedding. She also makes several copies of the service to be distributed to the wedding director, musicians, the engaged couple, and the minister(s).

Normally, the minister will give you the "Wedding Sourcebook Worksheet." If, however, you receive the completed worksheet directly from the engaged couple, be sure that the minister has approved the service.

When you are ready to type the wedding service, begin by typing the pertinent information at the top of the service, such as the names of the ones to be married, the date, time, and place of the wedding. Then follow the choices given by the couple on the "Wedding Sourcebook Worksheet." For instance, if the couple chooses Selection D in Category 1, turn to the Category 1 selections in part 1 and type that selection. Continue in the same manner through the service. If the couple chooses to omit a category, go to the next category and resume typing. Many of the services will have selections that have a blank space for the names of the couple. Consult the "Wedding Sourcebook Worksheet" to see how the couple prefers to be addressed in the wedding.

Part I

Designing
Your Own
Wedding

Instruction Page

Before you start choosing selections for your wedding, turn to part 2 and read through a couple of the original wedding services from the various Protestant churches. If you are a Presbyterian, for instance, read through the Presbyterian services. If one of you is Lutheran and the other Methodist, read through the Lutheran and Methodist services to get a feel for your traditions.

Once you think you have a feel for your tradition, and wedding services in general, use the "Wedding Sourcebook Worksheet" (pp. 19–20), and begin reading through the different selections for each category. (Sample worksheets have been filled out and are in the back of this book. Sample wedding services, using the instructions of the worksheets, are also in the back of the book.) Most of these selections are either direct portions of an existing Protestant service or a modified version of one of the original services. If you are curious as to the source of the selections, check the notes (pp. 83–86), where the sources are given.

At first, you may be overwhelmed with the choices within a particular category. Ordinarily, the selection process is not something you can do in one sitting. Many times it takes several sittings and much conversation between the two of you in order to choose the most meaningful selections for your service. It may be, in some cases, that you will find yourselves unable to decide among several selections. Don't panic! Make a note of them and discuss your options with your minister when you have completed the worksheet. Your minister will have helpful insights and suggestions.

Bear in mind that your minister is the final editor of your wedding service. He or she has been empowered by your church to perform the wedding ceremony and is ultimately responsible for the content and form of any wedding service. He or she has a responsibility not only to you but to the congregation to practice and uphold the governmental and theological positions of the church.

Traditional Wedding Service Order

1. **Opening Statement**
   "Dearly beloved, we are assembled here . . ."
   "Friends, we are gathered together . . ."

2. **Address to the Couple and/or Scripture Reading(s)**
   "Marriage is appointed that there may be lifelong companionship . . ."
   "Love is patient and kind . . ."

3. **Opening Prayer**
   "Look with favor upon these your servants . . ."
   "We thank you for the institution of marriage . . ."

4. **Questions of Intent**
   "Will you have this man to be your wedded . . . ?"
   "Will you love her, keep her . . . ?"

5. **Leavetaking**
   "Who presents this woman to be married to this man?" . . .
   "Do you give your blessings to . . . ?"

6. **The Vows**
   "I, _____, take you,
   _____, to be my . . ."
   "In sickness and in health . . ."

7. **Exchange of Rings**
   "With this ring, I thee wed . . ."
   "This ring I give you . . ."

8. **Declaration of Marriage**
   "I pronounce them husband and wife . . ."
   "What God has joined together . . ."

9. **Prayer for the Marriage**
   "Send your blessings upon . . ."
   "Grant them grace to live . . ."

10. **The Lord's Prayer**
    "Our Father, who art in heaven . . ."
    "Forgive us our sins . . ."

11. **Benediction**
    "Lift up his countenance upon you . . ."
    "In the name of the Father, the Son . . ."

Wedding Sourcebook Worksheet

WEDDING SERVICE
for

GROOM'S FULL NAME:

How would you like to be addressed in the wedding service (i.e., Jonathan, John, John William, etc.)?

BRIDE'S FULL NAME:

How would you like to be addressed in the wedding service (i.e., Catherine, Emily Catherine, Cathy, etc.)?

Date of the wedding: _____
Time: _____

Date of the rehearsal: _____
Time: _____

Place of the wedding: _____

Below, write in the selection letter you have chosen for each category. For instance, if you have chosen Selection D under Category 1, then fill in the blank with that letter in Category 1. Completed samples of this worksheet can be found in the back of the book (see pp. 178–179, 183–184).

❏ **CATEGORY 1: OPENING STATEMENT**

   Selection _____

❏ **CATEGORY 2: ADDRESS TO THE COUPLE AND/OR SCRIPTURE READING(S)**

(This category is optional. Some opening statements already contain words that address the couple, and redundancy is possible. A scripture reading or readings may be selected; if you wish to use one or more scripture readings here, write "O" in the blank below. A list of suggested scripture readings is given on p. 177.)

   Selection _____

(If you choose Selection O, list your scripture text[s] here.)

Scripture text(s) _____
_____
_____

❏ **CATEGORY 3: OPENING PRAYER**

   Selection _____

❏ **CATEGORY 4: QUESTIONS OF INTENT**

   Selection _____

❏ **CATEGORY 5: LEAVETAKING**

(This section is optional and may be omitted. You can choose a selection, omit the category, or, in consultation with the minister, write your own response.)

   Selection _____

We suggest this response:

_____

We choose to omit this section [ ]

❏ **CATEGORY 6: THE VOWS**

   Selection _____

❏ **CATEGORY 7: EXCHANGE OF RINGS**

   Selection _____

❏ **CATEGORY 8: DECLARATION OF MARRIAGE**

   Selection _____

❏ CATEGORY 9: PRAYER FOR THE MARRIAGE

(You may wish to include more than one prayer. If this is your desire, fill in more than one blank.)

Selection   _____   _____   _____

❏ CATEGORY 10: THE LORD'S PRAYER

(It is wise to choose the rendition of the Lord's Prayer that is most familiar to the worshiping congregation that will be in attendance at your wedding. Consult your minister if you are unsure about this. Or, you may have the Lord's Prayer sung by a soloist.)

Selection _____

The Lord's Prayer will be sung [   ]

Soloist's name: _____

❏ CATEGORY 10A: SPECIAL MUSIC

(Special music may be inserted here. If you plan to have special music as part of your service, indicate the title of the piece and the one singing or playing. In most cases, you would not want special music in this location if the Lord's Prayer is being sung.)

Special music title(s):

_____

_____

Performed by: _____

❏ CATEGORY 11: BENEDICTION

Selection

Special Music Note

In addition to Category 10a, there are other places in the wedding service where special music may be appropriate. One such place is after Category 4 (or 5), just prior to the vows. It is also traditional in some congregations to sing hymns during the wedding, and this is ordinarily done at the beginning of the service. However, you may wish to have music in another place in the service. If you desire to have other special music within the service, or to have congregational hymns, please indicate your wish here:

We would like to have additional special music after category _____

Title: _____

Performed by: _____

We would like to include a congregational hymn(s) after category _____

Hymn title(s): _____

_____

Are there other suggestions, concerns, or questions you have about your wedding service? If so, please indicate them in the following space:

_____

_____

_____

_____

_____

_____

_____

After you complete this worksheet, you will need to go through it with your minister. He or she may have other suggestions that will enhance the meaning and beauty of your service. After the minister has approved the service, *you may need to make arrangements to have the wedding service typed. Normally, the church secretary will be able to type it and have it ready before the rehearsal date. Confer with the minister or church secretary about this.*

Helpful Insights in Examining the Selections

Category 1: Opening Statement

Some of the opening statements conclude with a warning stating, "If anyone can show just cause why [this couple] may not be lawfully joined together, let them now speak, or else hereafter forever hold their peace." This line has added a certain drama to Hollywood's marriage scenes as we sit on the edge of our seat wondering if some disenchanted or broken-hearted lover is going to blurt out his or her protest. Yet this line adds little, if anything, to most of our wedding celebrations.

It is said that this line performed a necessary function in frontier days. The preacher wanted to make sure that neither the groom nor the bride had another spouse back in another territory!

Most traditional services contain such a warning; most contemporary services omit it.

Most traditional services begin, "Dearly beloved . . ." Other services begin with "Friends" or no address at all. Do not let this address become a stumbling block in choosing a particular selection that you might otherwise choose. Simply make a note on the "Wedding Sourcebook Worksheet" stating your desire to substitute one word for another.

Category 2: Address to the Couple and/or Scripture Reading(s)

Most traditional wedding services have a line that reads, "I require and charge you both, as you stand in the presence of God . . ." Many of the more recent services do not contain such a charge and contain another form of address to the couple in the opening statement. When choosing this selection, be careful that there is no duplication between the address and the opening statement. Making your selection for Category 2 is the trickiest of all choices and requires your most careful attention.

More and more wedding services are including scripture readings as part of the service. Indeed, the Old and New Testaments have pertinent words for this occasion. There is a list of appropriate scripture passages on p. 177. If you would like to include one or more of these texts, read through the suggested passages or consult your minister for his or her advice.

Category 5: Leavetaking

The traditional services provide for the "giving away" of the bride by the father. The question is asked, "Who gives this woman to be married to this man?" The father, or another family representative, answers, "I do" or "Her mother and I." In recent years some services have changed the question to "Who presents . . . ?" thereby changing the imagery that the woman is one who is "owned" by the parents.

The most recent trend has been to ask both families, not just the bride's, to give their blessing and support to the marriage. Therefore, the question is: "Do you give your blessing to _____ and _____, and promise to do everything in your power to uphold them in their marriage?" Both families then respond.

Some couples choose to omit this category altogether, especially if there has been a previous marriage. However, children of previous marriages are often incorporated into the service at this point and are asked the questions of blessing and support. In this category you will find a variety of selections to suit most circumstances.

Category 6: The Vows

There are a lot of options in the vows of the wedding service. Some of the selections are short, others long. There is also an option to answer "I do" to the minister's phrasing of the vows.

Category 7: Exchange of Rings

It is now fairly traditional in American culture for the bride and the groom to exchange rings. At one time it was more common for just the bride to receive a ring. In other cultures, such as those of some Native Americans, couples exchange symbols other than rings.

Category 10: The Lord's Prayer

The difference in the saying of the Lord's Prayer is among those who say "forgive us our debts, as we forgive our debtors," as opposed to those who say "forgive us our trespasses, as we forgive those who trespass against us"; or those who end the prayer with "forever," as opposed to those who say "forever and ever." Some churches may use the new ecumenical rendition that says "forgive us our sins . . ." It is important to either use the rendition that is traditional in your church or provide fellow worshipers with copies of the alternative version you have chosen.

Category 1:
Opening Statement

Selection A

The persons to be married stand before the minister with the man to the right of the woman. The minister shall say:

Our help is in the name of the Lord who made heaven and earth. Amen.

One of the following or another appropriate scriptural passage shall be read.

I will sing of the Lord's great love forever;
   with my mouth I will make your faithfulness
      known to all generations.
I will declare that your love stands firm forever,
   that you established your faithfulness in heaven
      itself. (Psalm 89:1–2)

or

O servants of the Lord,
you that stand in the house of the Lord,
   in the courts of the house of our God!
Praise the Lord, for the Lord is good;
   sing to his name, for he is gracious!
                              (Psalm 135:1b–3)

or

Grace and peace be yours in fullest measure, through the knowledge of God and Jesus our Lord. Amen. (2 Peter 1:2)

After the people have been seated, the minister shall say:

We are gathered here to praise God for the covenant of grace and reconciliation made with us through Jesus Christ, to hear it proclaimed anew, and to respond to it as we witness the covenant of marriage _____ and _____ make with each other in Christ's name.

Christian marriage is a joyful covenanting between a man and a woman in which they proclaim, before God and human witnesses, their commitment to live together in spiritual, physical, and material unity. In this covenant they acknowledge that the great love God has shown for each of them enables them to love each other. They affirm that God's gracious presence and abiding power are needed for them to keep their vows, to continue to live in love, and to be faithful servants of Christ in this world. For human commitment is fragile and human love imperfect, but the promise of God is eternal and the love of God can bring our love to perfection.

Selection B

The persons to be married stand before the minister with the man to the right of the woman. The minister shall say:

Friends, we are gathered together here in the presence of God and in the fellowship of this Christian community to join together _____ and _____ in Christian marriage. Christian marriage is a covenant of faith and trust between a man and woman, established within their shared commitment in the covenant of faith in Jesus Christ as Lord. Therefore, it requires of both man and woman:

openness of life and thought
> freedom from doubt and suspicion,
>> and
>>> commitment to speak the truth in love
>>>> as they grow into Christ
>>>>> who is the head of the church.

Christian marriage, furthermore, is a covenant of hope that endures all things and in which both husband and wife commit themselves to interpret each other's behavior with understanding and compassion, never giving up trying to communicate with each other.

Christian marriage, therefore, is a covenant of love in which both husband and wife empty themselves of their own concerns and take upon themselves the concerns of each other in loving each other as Christ loved the church and gave himself for it.

Therefore, this covenant is not to be entered into unadvisedly or lightly, but reverently, discreetly, advisedly, and in awe of God.

Into this holy union these two persons come now to be joined.

Selection C

The persons to be married stand before the minister with the man to the right of the woman. The minister shall say:

God is love, and those who abide in love abide in God, and God abides in them.

(1 John 4:16)

or

This is the day the Lord has made.
Let us rejoice and be glad in it.

(Psalm 118:24)

We have gathered in the presence of God
to give thanks for the gift of marriage,

to witness the joining together of _____
and _____,
to surround them with our prayers,
and to ask God's blessing upon them,
so that they may be strengthened for their life together
and nurtured in their love of God.

God created us male and female,
and gave us marriage
so that husband and wife may help and comfort each other,
living faithfully together in plenty and in want,
in joy and sorrow,
in sickness and in health,
throughout all their days.

God gave us marriage
for the full expression of the love between a man and a woman.
In marriage, a woman and a man belong to each other,
and with affection and tenderness
freely give themselves to each other.

God gave us marriage
for the well-being of human society,
for the ordering of family life,
and for the birth and nurture of children.

God gave us marriage as a holy mystery
in which a man and a woman are joined together
and become one,
just as Christ is one with the church.

Selection D

The persons to be married stand before the minister with the man to the right of the woman. The minister shall say:

Grace to you and peace
from God our Father and the Lord Jesus Christ.

(Romans 1:7)

or

Minister:

The Lord be with you.

People:

And also with you.

We have come together in the presence of God
to witness the marriage of
_____ and _____,
to surround them with our prayers,
and to share in their joy.

> *The minister calls the people to worship with one or more scriptural sentences, such as:*

Come, let us sing to the Lord;
let us come before his presence with thanksgiving.
(Psalm 95:1–2)

Give thanks to the Lord, for he is good;
his mercy endures for ever. (Psalm 118:1)

This is the day which the Lord has made;
let us rejoice and be glad in it. (Psalm 118:24)

God is love,
and those who live in love live in God,
and God lives in them. (1 John 4:16)

> *The minister says:*

Marriage is appointed by God.
The church believes that marriage
is a gift of God in creation
and a means of grace in which man and woman
become one in heart, mind, and body.

Marriage is the sacred and lifelong union
of a man and a woman
who give themselves to each other in love and trust.
It signifies the mystery of the union
between Christ and the church.

Marriage is given that husband and wife
may enrich and encourage each other
in every part of their life together.

Marriage is given that with delight and tenderness
they may know each other in love,
and through their physical union
may strengthen the union of their lives.

Marriage is given that children may be born
and brought up in security and love,
that home and family life may be strengthened,
and that society may stand upon firm foundations.

Marriage is a way of life which all people should
  honor;
it is not to be entered into lightly or selfishly,
but responsibly and in the love of God.

_____ and _____ are now to
  begin this way of life
which God has created and Christ has blessed.
Therefore, on this their wedding day, we pray for
  them,
asking that they may fulfill God's purpose
for the whole of their lives.

Selection E

> *The persons to be married stand before the minister with the man to the right of the woman. The minister shall say:*

Dearly beloved, we are gathered together here in the
sight of God, and in the presence of these witnesses,
to join together _____ and _____
in holy matrimony: which is an honorable estate, instituted of God, and signifying unto us the mystical
union which exists between Christ and his church;
which holy estate Christ adorned and beautified with
his presence in Cana of Galilee. It is therefore not
to be entered into unadvisedly, but reverently, discreetly, and in awe of God. Into this holy estate these
two persons come now to be joined.

Selection F

> *The persons to be married stand before the minister with the man to the right of the woman. The minister shall say:*

The grace of our Lord Jesus Christ and the love of
God and the communion of the Holy Spirit be with
you all.

> *and/or*

Love comes from God. Everyone who truly loves is
a child of God. Let us worship God.

Dearly beloved, we are gathered here as the people of God to witness the marriage of _____ and _____.

We come to share in their joy and to ask God to bless them. Marriage is a gift of God, sealed by a sacred covenant. God gives human love. Through that love, husband and wife come to know each other with mutual care and companionship. God gives joy. Through that joy, wife and husband may share their new life with others as Jesus shared new wine at the wedding in Cana.

With our love and our prayers, we support _____ and _____ as they now freely give themselves to each other.

Selection G

The persons to be married stand before the minister with the man to the right of the woman. The minister shall say:

The grace of our Lord Jesus Christ and the love of God and the communion of the Holy Spirit be with you all.

and/or

Love comes from God. Everyone who truly loves is a child of God. Let us worship God.

Dear friends, we have come together in the presence of God to witness the marriage of _____ and _____, to surround them with our prayers, and to share in their joy.

The scriptures teach us that the bond and covenant of marriage is a gift of God, a holy mystery in which man and woman become one flesh, an image of the union of Christ and the church.

As this woman and this man give themselves to each other today, we remember that at Cana in Galilee our Savior Jesus Christ made the wedding feast a sign of God's reign of love.

Let us enter into this celebration confident that through the Holy Spirit, Christ is present with us now. We pray that this couple may fulfill God's purpose for the whole of their lives.

Selection H

The persons to be married stand before the minister with the man to the right of the woman. The minister shall say:

Dearly beloved: We have come together in the presence of God to witness and bless the joining together of _____ and _____ in holy matrimony. The bond and covenant of marriage was established by God in creation, and our Lord Jesus Christ adorned this manner of life by his presence and first miracle at a wedding in Cana of Galilee. It signifies to us the mystery of the union between Christ and his church, and Holy Scripture commends it to be honored among all people.

The union of husband and wife in heart, body, and mind is intended by God for their mutual joy; for the help and comfort given one another in prosperity and adversity; and, when it is God's will, for the procreation of children and their nurture in the knowledge and love of the Lord. Therefore marriage is not to be entered into unadvisedly or lightly, but reverently, deliberately, and in accordance with the purposes for which it was instituted by God.

Into this holy union _____ and _____ now come to be joined.

Selection I

The persons to be married shall present themselves before the minister, the man standing at the right hand of the woman. Then the minister shall say:

Dearly beloved, we are assembled here in the presence of God, to join _____ and _____ in holy marriage; which is instituted by God, regulated by his commandments, blessed by our Lord Jesus Christ, and to be held in honor among all people. Let us therefore reverently remember that God has established and sanctified marriage, for the welfare and happiness of humankind. Our Savior has declared that a man shall leave his father and mother and be faithful to his wife. By his apostles, he has instructed those who enter into this relation to cherish a mutual esteem and love; to bear with each other's infirmities and weaknesses; to comfort each other in sickness, trouble, and sorrow; in honesty and industry to provide for each other, and for their household, in temporal things; to pray for and encourage each other in the things which pertain to God; and to live together as the heirs of the grace of life.

Selection J

The persons to be married stand before the minister with the man to the right of the woman. The minister shall say:

In the Name of the Father, and of the Son, and of the Holy Ghost. Amen.

Dearly beloved: In that marriage is a holy union, ordained of God, and to be held in honor by all, it is fitting to those who enter marriage to weigh, with reverent minds, what the Word of God teaches concerning it: The Lord God said, It is not good that the man should live alone; I will make a suitable companion.... Our Lord Jesus Christ said: Haven't you read the scripture that says that in the beginning the Creator made people male and female? And God said, For this reason a man will leave his father and mother and unite with his wife, and the two will become one. So they are no longer two, but one. Man must not separate, then, what God has joined together.

The Apostle Paul, speaking of marriage, said: Submit yourselves to one another because of your reverence to Christ.

In that marriage is a union that is holy and acceptable to God, he is ever present with his abundant blessing. Into this holy union, _____ and _____ come now to be joined.

Selection K

The persons to be married stand before the minister with the man to the right of the woman. The minister shall say:

Our help is in the name of the Lord, who made heaven and earth.

Then the minister shall say to all present:

Dearly beloved, we are assembled here in the sight of God and in the presence of this company to join _____ and _____ in the bonds of holy marriage; which is an honorable estate, instituted by God when he said that a man shall leave his father and his mother and shall be joined to his wife; and they shall be one flesh. It was confirmed by the words of our blessed Savior; made holy by his presence at the marriage in Cana of Galilee, and compared by St. Paul to the mystical union between Christ and his church. It ought not, therefore, be entered into lightly or hastily, but reverently, discreetly, and in awe of God.

These two persons have come to be joined into this holy estate.

Selection L

At the appointed time, the man and the woman to be married shall stand before the minister, the man at the right hand of the woman, when the minister shall say:

Our help is in the name of the Lord, who made heaven and earth.

Then the minister shall say to all present:

Dearly beloved, we are assembled here in the sight of God and in the presence of this company to join _____ and _____ in the bonds of holy marriage; which is an honorable estate, instituted by God when he said that a man shall leave his father and his mother and shall cleave to his wife; and they shall be one flesh. It was confirmed by the words of our blessed Savior; hallowed by his presence at the marriage in Cana of Galilee, and compared by St. Paul to the mystical union between Christ and his church. It ought not, therefore, be entered into lightly or hastily, but reverently, discreetly, and in the fear of God.

These two persons have come to be joined into this holy estate. If anyone, therefore, can show just cause why they may not lawfully be joined together, let them now declare it, or else hereafter hold their peace.

Selection M

The persons to be married stand before the minister with the man to the right of the woman. The minister shall say:

Dearly beloved, we are gathered together here in the sight of God, and in the presence of these witnesses, to join together _____ and _____ in holy matrimony: which is an honorable estate, instituted of God, and signifying unto us the mystical union which exists between Christ and his church; which holy estate Christ adorned and beautified with his presence in Cana of Galilee. It is therefore not to be entered into unadvisedly, but reverently, discreetly, and in the fear of God. Into this holy estate these two persons come now to be joined.

Selection N

The persons to be married stand before the minister with the man to the right of the woman. The minister shall say:

Dearly beloved: We have come together in the presence of God to witness and bless the joining together of _____ and _____ in holy matrimony. The bond and covenant of marriage was established by God in creation, and our Lord Jesus Christ adorned this manner of life by his presence and first miracle at a wedding in Cana of Galilee. It signifies to us the mystery of the union between Christ and his church, and Holy Scripture commends it to be honored among all people.

The union of husband and wife in heart, body, and mind is intended by God for their mutual joy; for the help and comfort given one another in prosperity and adversity; and, when it is God's will, for the procreation of children and their nurture in the knowledge and love of the Lord. Therefore marriage is not to be entered into unadvisedly or lightly, but reverently, deliberately, and in accordance with the purposes for which it was instituted by God.

Into this holy union _____ and _____ now come to be joined. If any of you can show just cause why they may not lawfully be married, speak now; or else for ever hold your peace.

Selection O

The persons to be married shall present themselves before the minister, the man standing at the right hand of the woman. Then the minister shall say:

Dearly beloved, we are assembled here in the presence of God, to join _____ and _____ in holy marriage; which is instituted by God, regulated by his commandments, blessed by our Lord Jesus Christ, and to be held in honor among all people. Let us therefore reverently remember that God has established and sanctified marriage, for the welfare and happiness of humankind. Our Savior has declared that a man shall leave his father and mother and be faithful to his wife. By his apostles, he has instructed those who enter into this relation to cherish a mutual esteem and love; to bear with each other's infirmities and weaknesses; to comfort each other in sickness, trouble, and sorrow; in honesty and industry to provide for each other, and for their household, in temporal things; to pray for and encourage each other in the things which pertain to God; and to live together as the heirs of the grace of life.

Forasmuch as these two persons have come to be made one in this holy estate, if there be any here present who knows any just cause why they may not lawfully be joined in marriage, I require them now to make it known, or ever after to hold their peace.

Selection P

The persons to be married present themselves before the minister, the man standing at the right hand of the woman. The minister says:

Dearly beloved, we are gathered here in the presence of God to join this man and this woman in marriage. This is a way of life instituted by God, and Holy Scripture commands all people to hold it in honor. Our Lord Jesus Christ blessed it by his presence at Cana of Galilee.

About this way of life, hear what our Lord says:

> From the beginning of creation, "God made them male and female." "For this reason a man shall leave his father and mother and be joined to his wife, and the two shall become one." So they are no longer two but one. What therefore God has joined together, let not man put asunder. (Mark 10:6–9)

Marriage is therefore not by any to be undertaken lightly or ill-advisedly, but seriously and prayerfully, duly considering the purpose for which it is ordained.

It is ordained:

> That husband and wife may give to each other life-long companionship, help, and comfort, both in prosperity and in adversity;

> That God may hallow and direct the natural instincts and affections created by himself, and redeemed in Christ;

> That children may be born and brought up in families in the knowledge of our Lord Jesus Christ to the glory of God;

> That, marriage being thus held in honor, human society may stand upon firm foundations.

Selection Q

The persons to be married present themselves before the minister, the man standing at the right hand of the woman. The minister says:

Dearly beloved, we are gathered here in the presence of God to join this man and this woman in marriage. This is a way of life instituted by God, and Holy Scripture commands all people to hold it in honor. Our Lord Jesus Christ blessed it by his presence at Cana of Galilee.

About this way of life, hear what our Lord says:

> From the beginning of creation, "God made them male and female." "For this reason a man shall leave his father and mother and be joined to his wife, and the two shall become one." So they are no longer two but one. What therefore God has

joined together, let not man put asunder. (Mark 10:6–9)

Marriage is therefore not by any to be undertaken lightly or ill-advisedly, but seriously and prayerfully, duly considering the purpose for which it is ordained.

It is ordained:

> That husband and wife may give to each other life-long companionship, help, and comfort, both in prosperity and in adversity;

> That God may hallow and direct the natural instincts and affections created by himself, and redeemed in Christ;

> That, marriage being thus held in honor, human society may stand upon firm foundations.

Selection R

The persons to be married present themselves before the minister, the man standing at the right hand of the woman. The minister shall say:

In the name of the Father, and of the Son, and of the Holy Spirit. Amen.

or

Our help is in the name of the Lord who made heaven and earth. Amen.

Dearly beloved, we are gathered together in the sight of God to join _____ and _____ in marriage. Let all who enter it know that marriage is a sacred and joyous covenant, a way of life ordained of God from the beginning of his creation. "For this reason," says the Lord, "a man shall leave his father and mother and be joined to his wife, and the two shall become one flesh. What therefore God has joined together, let no man put asunder." Marriage is also compared by the apostle Paul to the mystical union between Christ and his church. Therefore, it should not be entered into unadvisedly or lightly, but reverently, considering the purposes for which it was ordained.

God has ordered the covenant of marriage: that husband and wife may give to each other companionship, help, and comfort, both in prosperity and in adversity; that he may hallow the expression of the natural affections, that children may be born and nurtured in families and trained in godliness; and that human society may stand on firm foundations.

Into this sacred covenant these two persons now desire to enter.

Selection S

The persons to be married stand before the minister with the man to the right of the woman. The minister shall say:

Dearly beloved, we are gathered together here in the sight of God, and in the presence of these witnesses, to join together _____ and _____ in holy matrimony: which is an honorable estate, instituted of God, and signifying unto us the mystical union which exists between Christ and his church; which holy estate Christ adorned and beautified with his presence in Cana of Galilee. It is therefore not to be entered into unadvisedly, but reverently, discreetly, and in the fear of God. Into this holy estate these two persons come now to be joined. If anyone can show just cause why they may not lawfully be joined together, let them now speak, or else hereafter forever hold their peace.

Selection T

The persons to be married stand before the minister with the man standing to the right of the woman. The minister shall say:

Dearly beloved, we are here assembled, in the presence of God and these witnesses, to join together this man, _____, and this woman, _____, in holy marriage, which is blessed by our Lord Jesus Christ, governed by God's commandments, and is to be held in honor among all people. Therefore it is not to be entered into unadvisedly or lightly, but reverently, discreetly, and in the fear of God.

In Holy Scripture we are taught:

That marriage was instituted by God himself, and is therefore a holy estate; that, according to the ordinance of God, a man and his wife, shall be one flesh; that, under the New Covenant, the married state has been sanctified to be an emblem of Christ and his church; that the husband, as the head of the wife, should love her, even as Christ also loved the church; and that the wife be subject to her own husband in the Lord, as the church is subject unto Christ; that, in consequence, Christians thus united together should love one another, as one in the Lord, be faithful one to the other, bear with each other's infirmities and weaknesses, cherish each other in joy and sorrow, pray for and encourage each other in all things, and live together as heirs of the grace of life.

Into this holy estate these two persons come now to be joined. If any man can show just cause why they may not lawfully be joined together, according to the Word of God and the laws of this State, let him now speak, or else forever hold his peace.

Selection U

The persons to be married stand before the minister with the man standing to the right of the woman. The minister shall say:

Dearly beloved, we are here assembled, in the presence of God and these witnesses, to join together this man, _____, and this woman, _____, in holy marriage, which is blessed by our Lord Jesus Christ, governed by God's commandments, and is to be held in honor among all people. Therefore it is not to be entered into unadvisedly or lightly, but reverently, discreetly, and in awe of God.

In Holy Scripture we are taught:

That marriage was instituted by God himself, and is therefore a holy estate; that, according to the ordinance of God, a man and his wife, shall be one flesh; that, under the New Covenant, the married state has been sanctified to be an emblem of Christ and his church; that the husband and the wife be subject to one another out of reverence to Christ. That, in consequence, Christians thus united together should love one another, as one in the Lord, be faithful one to the other, bear with each other's infirmities and weaknesses, cherish each other in joy and sorrow, pray for and encourage each other in all things, and live together as heirs of the grace of life.

Into this holy estate these two persons come now to be joined.

Selection V

The persons to be married stand before the minister with the man to the right of the woman. The minister shall say:

Dearly beloved, we are gathered here in the presence of God to join together _____ and _____ in holy matrimony; which is an honorable estate, ordained of God unto the fulfilling and perfecting of the love of man and woman in mutual honor and forbearance; and therefore it is not by any to be taken in hand lightly, or thoughtlessly, but reverently, discreetly, soberly, and in the fear of God.

Into which holy estate these two persons present come now to be joined.

Therefore if any man can show just cause, why they may not lawfully be joined together, let him now speak, or else hereafter for ever hold his peace.

Selection W

The persons to be married stand before the minister with the man to the right of the woman. The minister shall say:

Dearly beloved, we are gathered here in the presence of God to join together _____ and _____ in holy matrimony; which is an honorable estate, ordained of God unto the fulfilling and perfecting of the love of man and woman in mutual honor and patience; and therefore it is not by any to be taken in hand lightly, or thoughtlessly, but reverently, discreetly, soberly, and in awe of God.

Into this holy estate these two persons present come now to be joined.

Selection X

The persons to be married stand before the minister with the man to the right of the woman. The minister shall say:

Unless the Lord builds the house, its builders will have toiled in vain.

Our help is in the name of the Lord, Maker of heaven and earth.

Beloved, we have come together in the house of God to celebrate the marriage of this man and this woman, in the assurance that the Lord Jesus Christ, whose power was revealed at the wedding in Cana of Galilee, is present with us here in all his power and his love.

Marriage is provided by God as part of his loving purpose for humanity since the beginning of creation. Jesus said, "The Creator made them from the beginning male and female. For this reason a man shall leave his father and mother, and be made one with his wife: and the two shall become one flesh."

Marriage is enriched by God for all who have faith in the gospel, for through the saving grace of Christ and the renewal of the Holy Spirit husband and wife can love one another as Christ loves them.

Marriage is thus a gift and calling of God and is not to be undertaken lightly or from selfish motives but with reverence and dedication, with faith in the enabling power of Christ, and with due awareness of the purpose for which it is appointed by God.

Marriage is appointed that there may be lifelong companionship, comfort, and joy between husband and wife.

It is appointed as the right and proper setting for the full expression of physical love between man and woman.

It is appointed for the ordering of family life, where children, . . . who are also God's gifts to us, . . . may enjoy the security of love and the heritage of faith.

It is appointed for the well-being of human society, which can be stable and happy only where the marriage bond is honored and upheld.

Then addressing the couple the minister shall say:

_____ and _____ you seek to be joined in marriage. I am required to ask you, if you know any reason why you may not lawfully be married to each other, to declare it now.

Selection Y

The persons to be married stand before the minister with the man to the right of the woman. The minister shall say:

Unless the Lord builds the house, its builders will have toiled in vain.

Our help is in the name of the Lord, Maker of heaven and earth.

Beloved, we have come together in the house of God to celebrate the marriage of _____ and _____, in the assurance that the Lord Jesus Christ, whose power was revealed at the wedding in Cana of Galilee, is present with us here in all his power and his love.

Marriage is provided by God as part of his loving purpose for humanity since the beginning of creation. Jesus said, "The Creator made them from the beginning male and female. For this reason a man shall leave his father and mother, and be made one with his wife: and the two shall become one flesh."

Marriage is enriched by God for all who have faith in the gospel, for through the saving grace of Christ and the renewal of the Holy Spirit husband and wife can love one another as Christ loves them.

Marriage is thus a gift and calling of God and is not to be undertaken lightly or from selfish motives but with reverence and dedication, with faith in the enabling power of Christ, and with due awareness of the purpose for which it is appointed by God.

Marriage is appointed that there may be lifelong companionship, comfort, and joy between husband and wife.

It is appointed as the right and proper setting for the full expression of physical love between man and woman.

It is appointed for the well-being of human society, which can be stable and happy only where the marriage bond is honored and upheld.

Selection Z

The persons to be married stand before the minister with the man to the right of the woman. The minister shall say:

Dearly beloved, we are gathered together here in the sight of God, and in the face of this company, to join together _____ and _____ in holy matrimony; which is an honorable estate, instituted of God, signifying unto us the mystical union that is between Christ and his church: which holy estate Christ adorned and beautified with his presence and first miracle that he performed in Cana of Galilee, and is commended of Saint Paul to be honorable among all people: and therefore is not by any to be entered into unadvisedly or lightly; but reverently, discreetly, advisedly, soberly, and in the fear of God. Into this holy estate these two persons present come now to be joined. If anyone can show just cause, why they may not lawfully be joined together, let them now speak, or else hereafter for ever hold their peace.

Selection AA

The persons to be married stand before the minister with the man to the right of the woman. The minister shall say:

Friends, we are gathered together here in the sight of God, and in the presence of this company, to join together _____ and _____ in holy marriage; which is an honorable estate, instituted of God, signifying unto us the mystical union that is between Christ and his church: which holy estate Christ adorned and beautified with his presence and first miracle that he performed in Cana of Galilee, and is commended of Saint Paul to be honorable among all people: and therefore is not by any to be entered into unadvisedly or lightly; but reverently, discreetly, advisedly, seriously, and in awe of God.

Into this holy estate these two persons present come now to be joined.

Selection BB

At the appointed time, with the man standing at the right hand of the woman, the minister shall say:

In the name of the Father, and of the Son, and of the Holy Spirit. Amen.

or

Our help is in the name of the Lord who made heaven and earth. Amen.

Dearly beloved, we are gathered together in the sight of God to join _____ and _____ in marriage. Let all who enter it know that marriage is a sacred and joyous covenant, a way of life ordained of God from the beginning of his creation. "For this reason," says the Lord, "a man shall leave his father and mother and be joined to his wife, and the two shall become one flesh. What therefore God has joined together, let no man put asunder." Marriage is also compared by the apostle Paul to the mystical union between Christ and his church. Therefore, it should not be entered into unadvisedly or lightly, but reverently, considering the purposes for which it was ordained.

God has ordered the covenant of marriage: that husband and wife may give to each other companionship, help, and comfort, both in prosperity and in adversity; that he may make holy the expression of the natural affections; and that human society may stand on firm foundations.

Into this sacred covenant these two persons now desire to enter.

Selection CC

The minister says:

As a community of friends, we are gathered here in God's presence to witness the marriage of _____ and _____, and to ask God to bless them.

We are called to rejoice in their happiness, to help them when they have trouble, and to remember them in our prayers. Marriage, like our creation as men and women, owes its existence to God. It is his will and purpose that a husband and wife should love each other throughout their life (and that children born to them should enjoy the security of family and home).

Selection DD

The minister says:

Friends, we are gathered together in the sight of God to witness and to bless the joining of _____ and _____ in Christian marriage. The covenant of marriage was established by God, who created us male and female for each other. With his presence and power, Jesus graced a wedding at Cana of Galilee and in his sacrificial love gave us the example for the love of husband and wife. _____ and _____ come to give themselves to one another in this holy covenant.

Category 2:
Address to the Couple and/or
Scripture Reading(s)

Selection A

The minister addresses the couple saying:

_____ and _____, your marriage is intended to join you for life in a relationship so intimate and personal that it will change your whole being. God offers you the hope, and indeed the promise, of a love that is true and mature.

Selection B

The minister addresses the couple saying:

I encourage you both to remember that:

Love is patient and kind;
love is not jealous or boastful;
it is not arrogant or rude.
Love does not insist on its own way;
it is not irritable or resentful;
it does not rejoice at wrong,
but rejoices in the right.

Love bears all things,
believes all things,
hopes all things,
endures all things.
        (1 Corinthians 13:4–7, RSV)

Selection C

The minister addresses the couple saying:

In marriage, husband and wife are called to a new
    way of life,
created, ordered, and blessed by God.
This way of life must not be entered into carelessly,
or from selfish motives,
but responsibly, and prayerfully.

We rejoice that marriage is given by God,
blessed by our Lord Jesus Christ,
and sustained by the Holy Spirit.
Therefore, let marriage be held in honor among all.

Selection D

The minister addresses the couple saying:

As God's picked representatives of the new humanity, purified and beloved of God himself, be merciful in action, kindly in heart, humble in mind. Accept life, and be most patient and tolerant with one another. Forgive as freely as the Lord has forgiven you. And, above everything else, be truly loving. Let the peace of Christ rule in your hearts, remembering that as members of the one body you are called to live in harmony, and never forget to be thankful for what God has done for you.

Selection E

The minister addresses the couple saying:

Love is slow to lose patience — it looks for a way of being constructive. It is not possessive; it is neither anxious to impress nor does it cherish inflated ideas of its own importance. Love has good manners and does not pursue selfish advantage. It is not touchy. It does not keep account of evil or gloat over the wickedness of other people. On the contrary, it is glad with all good people when truth prevails. Love knows no limit to its endurance, no end to its trust, no fading of its hope; it can outlast anything. It still stands when all else has fallen.

Selection F

The minister addresses the couple saying:

I require and charge you both, as you stand in the presence of God, before whom the secrets of all hearts are disclosed, that, having duly considered the holy covenant you are about to make, you do now declare before this company your pledge of faith, each to the other. Be well assured that if these solemn vows are kept inviolate, as God's Word demands, and if steadfastly you endeavor to do the will of your heavenly Father, God will bless your marriage, will grant you fulfillment in it, and will establish your home in peace.

Selection G

The minister addresses the couple saying:

I require and charge you both, as you stand in the presence of God, that, having duly considered the holy covenant you are about to make, you do now declare before this congregation your pledge of faith to one another. Be confident that if these solemn vows are kept unbroken, as God's Word demands, and if you seek to do the will of God, God will bless your marriage, will grant you fulfillment in it, and will establish your home in peace.

Selection H

The minister addresses the couple saying:

The Lord God in his goodness created us male and female, and by the gift of marriage founded human community in a joy that begins now and is brought to perfection in the life to come.

Because of sin, our age-old rebellion, the gladness of marriage can be overcast and the gift of the family can become a burden.

But because God, who established marriage, continues still to bless it with his abundant and ever-present support, we can be sustained in our weariness and have our joy restored.

Selection I

The minister addresses the couple saying:

God has ordered the covenant of marriage: that husband and wife may give to each other companionship, help, and comfort, both in prosperity and in adversity; that he may hallow the expression of the natural affections; that children may be born and nurtured in families and trained in godliness; and that human society may stand on firm foundations.

Selection J

The minister addresses the couple saying:

God has ordered the covenant of marriage: that husband and wife may give to each other companionship, help, and comfort, both in prosperity and in adversity; that he may make holy the expression of the natural affections; that children, if desired, may be born and nurtured in families and trained in the Christian faith; and that human society may stand on firm foundations.

Selection K

(Do not use this selection in conjunction with Selection X or Y in Category 1.)

The minister addresses the couple saying:

Marriage is appointed that there may be lifelong companionship, comfort, and joy between husband and wife.

It is appointed as the right and proper setting for the full expression of physical love between man and woman.

It is appointed for the ordering of family life, where children — who are also God's gifts to us — may enjoy the security of love and the heritage of faith.

It is appointed for the well-being of human society, which can be stable and happy only where the marriage bond is honored and upheld.

Selection L

(Do not use this selection in conjunction with Selection X or Y in Category 1.)

The minister addresses the couple saying:

Marriage is appointed that there may be lifelong companionship, comfort, and joy between husband and wife.

It is appointed as the right and proper setting for the full expression of physical love between man and woman.

It is appointed for the well-being of human society, which can be stable and happy only where the marriage bond is honored and upheld.

Selection M

The minister addresses the couple saying:

It is ordained:

That husband and wife may give to each other lifelong companionship, help, and comfort, both in prosperity and in adversity;

That God may hallow and direct the natural instincts and affections created by himself, and redeemed in Christ,

That children may be born and brought up in families in the knowledge of our Lord Jesus Christ to the glory of God;

That, marriage being thus held in honor, human society may stand upon firm foundations.

Selection N

The minister addresses the couple saying:

It is ordained:

That husband and wife may give to each other lifelong companionship, help, and comfort, both in prosperity and in adversity;

That God may make holy and direct the natural instincts and affections created by himself, and redeemed in Christ;

That children may be born or adopted and brought up in families in the knowledge of our Lord Jesus Christ to the glory of God;

That, marriage being thus held in honor, human society may stand upon firm foundations.

Selection O

Scripture reading(s). Old and New Testament lessons may be included in the wedding and can be inserted at this point in the service. For a list of suggested scripture passages for a wedding service, turn to page 177. If you chose one or more of these scriptures, list them on your worksheet under Category 2. Be careful, however, that you do not duplicate a particular scripture. Some opening statements in Category 1 contain scripture passages. Note also that Selection B in this category is a New Testament passage from 1 Corinthians 13.

Category 3:
Opening Prayer

Selection A

The minister says:

Let us pray.

Almighty and eternal God, giver of all good gifts, look with favor, we pray, on these your servants who lift up their hearts to you. Enable them to make their vows to one another in all sincerity, as in your sight, and to be faithful in keeping them, to the glory of your holy name; through Jesus Christ our Lord. Amen.

Selection B

The minister says:

Let us pray.

Gracious God,
you are always faithful in your love for us.
Look mercifully upon _____ and

_____,
who have come seeking your blessing.
Let your Holy Spirit rest upon them
so that with steadfast love
they may honor the promises they make this day,
through Jesus Christ our Savior.

Amen.

Selection C

The minister says:

Let us pray.

Almighty and most merciful Father, we your unworthy children praise you for all the bounties of your providence, and for all the gifts of your grace. We thank you especially for the institution of marriage, which you have ordained to guard, to hallow, and to perfect the gift of love. We thank you for the joy which these your servants find in each other, and for the love and trust in which they enter this holy covenant. And since without your help we cannot do anything as we ought, we pray you to enrich your servants with your grace, that they may enter into their marriage as in your sight, and truly keep their vows; through Jesus Christ our Lord. Amen.

Selection D

The minister says:

Let us pray.

Almighty and ever-blessed God, whose presence is the happiness of every condition, and whose favor hallows every relation: We ask you to be present and favorable to these your servants, that they may be truly joined in the honorable estate of marriage, in the covenant of their God. As you have brought them together by your providence, sanctify them by your

Spirit, giving them a new frame of heart fit for their new life; and enrich them with all grace, whereby they may enjoy the comforts, undergo the cares, endure the trials, and perform the duties of life together as Christians, under your divine guidance and protection; through our Lord Jesus Christ. Amen.

Selection E

The minister says:

Let us pray.

Almighty Father, Lord of heaven and earth, we praise you for your goodness and for your many gifts. Your power created us, your Son redeemed us, your Spirit sets us free to love. For the richness and variety of life; for the providence which guides us and directs our path; and for the happiness of deep relationships with one another, we give thanks to you. Especially today we bless you for the gift of marriage, by which human love is hallowed and made perfect. For the joy that _____ and _____ have found in one another, and for the love and trust in which they enter this covenant of marriage, we give thanks to you, Lord God.

Give them your Spirit that the vows they make to one another in your presence may be the beginning of a true and lifelong union. We ask this in the name of Jesus Christ, the Lord of life. Amen.

Selection F

The minister says:

Let us pray.

Almighty and most merciful Father, without whose help we cannot do anything as we ought, we pray that, as you have brought these persons together by your providence, you will enrich them with your grace, that they may enter into the marriage covenant as in your sight, and truly keep the vows they are about to make; through Jesus Christ our Lord. Amen.

Selection G

The minister says:

Let us pray.

O gracious and ever-living God, you have created us male and female in your image: Look mercifully upon this man and this woman who come to you seeking your blessing, and assist them with your grace, that with true fidelity and steadfast love they may honor and keep the promises and vows they make; through Jesus Christ our Savior, who lives and reigns with you in the unity of the Holy Spirit, for ever and ever. Amen.

Selection H

The minister says:

Let us pray.

To you, almighty and most merciful God, we come this day; for we know our happiness is incomplete until we are found by you, and that our relationships with each other, and with all persons, hinge on our relationship with you. Be present, God, with all of us in this hour, that these two persons may be filled with love and the gift of life, and that all of us may receive a newness of life which only becomes real through our being joined to you. As you have brought these two persons together, inspire them by your Spirit, give them a new frame of heart fit for their new relationship, and enrich them with all grace, that they may enjoy the comforts, undergo the cares, endure the trials, and perform the duties of life together, as persons committed to the Lord Jesus Christ, in whose name we pray. Amen.

Selection I

The minister says:

Let us pray.

Eternal God, as you gladdened the wedding at Cana in Galilee by the presence of your Son, Jesus, so by his presence now make the occasion of this wedding one of rejoicing. In your favor look upon

_____ and _____, about to be joined in marriage, and grant that they might enjoy love and happiness in their relationship, as they look to serve each other and you. Amen.

Selection J

The minister says:

Let us pray.

Gracious God, always faithful in your love for us, we rejoice in your presence. You create love. You unite us in one human family. You offer your word and lead us in light. You open your loving arms and embrace us with strength. May the presence of Christ fill our hearts with new joy and make new the lives of your servants whose marriage we celebrate. Bless all creation through this sign of your love shown in the love of _____ and _____ for each other. May the power of your Holy Spirit sustain them and all of us in love that knows no end. Amen.

Selection K

The minister says:

Let us pray.

Eternal God, our Creator and Redeemer, as you gladdened the wedding at Cana in Galilee by the presence of your Son, so by your presence now bring your joy to this wedding. In favor look upon this couple and grant that they, rejoicing in all your gifts, may at length celebrate with Christ the Bridegroom, the marriage feast which has no end. Amen.

Selection L

The minister says:

Let us pray.

Eternal God, our Creator and Redeemer, as you gladdened the wedding at Cana in Galilee by the presence of your Son, so by our presence now bring your joy to this wedding. In favor look upon this couple and grant that they, rejoicing in all your gifts, may

at length celebrate with Christ the marriage feast which has no end. Amen.

Selection M

The minister says:

Let us pray.

Eternal God,
creator and preserver of all life,
author of salvation, giver of all grace:
Bless and sanctify with your Holy Spirit
_____ and _____
who come now to join in marriage.
Grant that they may give their vows to each other
in the strength of your steadfast love.
Enable them to grow in love and peace
with you and with one another all their days,
that they may reach out
in concern and service to the world,
through Jesus Christ our Lord. Amen.

Selection N

The minister says:

Let us pray.

Gracious God,
your generous love surrounds us,
and everything we enjoy comes from you.
In your great love
you have given us the gift of marriage.
Bless _____ and _____ as they
    pledge their lives to each other;
that their love may continue to grow
and be the true reflection of your love for us all;
through Jesus Christ our Lord.
Amen.

Selection O

The minister says:

Father,
you have made the covenant of marriage a holy
    mystery,

a symbol of Christ's love for the church.
Hear our prayers for _____ and

_____.

With faith in you and in each other,
they pledge their love today.
May their lives always bear witness
to the reality of that love.
We ask this through your Son,
our Lord Jesus Christ.
Amen.

Selection P

The minister says:

Let us pray.

O God, we gather to celebrate your gift of love and its presence among us. We rejoice that two people have chosen to commit themselves to a life of loving faithfulness to one another. We praise you, O God, for the ways you have touched our lives with a variety of loving relationships. We give thanks that we have experienced your love through the life-giving love of Jesus Christ and through the care and affection of other people.

At the same time, we remember and confess to you, O God, that we often have failed to be loving, that we often have taken for granted the people for whom we care most. We selfishly neglect and strain the bonds that unite us with others.

We hurt those who love us and withdraw from the community that encircles us. Forgive us, O God. Renew within us an affectionate spirit. Enrich our lives with the gracious gift of your love so that we may embrace others with the same love. May our participation in this celebration of love and commitment give us a new joy and responsiveness to the relationships we cherish; through Jesus Christ we pray. Amen.

Through the great depth and strength of God's love for us, God reaches out to us to forgive our sins and to restore us to life. Be assured, children of God, that God's love enfolds us and upbuilds us so that we may continue to love one another as God has loved us.

Category 4:
Questions of Intent

Selection A

Then the minister, calling the man by his Christian name, shall say:

_____, will you have this woman to be your wife, and will you pledge yourself to her, in all love and honor, in all duty and service, in all faith and tenderness, to live with her, and cherish her, according to the ordinance of God, in the holy bond of marriage?

The man shall answer:

I will.

Then the minister, calling the woman by her Christian name, shall say:

_____, will you have this man to be your husband, and will you pledge yourself to him, in all love and honor, in all duty and service, in all faith and tenderness, to live with him, and cherish him, according to the ordinance of God, in the holy bond of marriage?

The woman shall answer:

I will.

Selection B

Then the minister, calling the man by his Christian name, shall say:

_____, will you have this woman to be your wife, and will you pledge your faithfulness to her, in all love and honor, in all duty and service, in all faith and tenderness, to live with her, and cherish her, according to the ordinance of God, in the holy bond of marriage?

The man shall answer:

I will.

Then the minister, calling the woman by her Christian name, shall say:

_____, will you have this man to be your husband, and will you pledge your faithfulness to him, in all love and honor, in all duty and service, in all faith and tenderness, to live with him, and cherish him, according to the ordinance of God, in the holy bond of marriage?

The woman shall answer:

I will.

Selection C

The minister addresses the groom:

_____, having heard how God honors the
covenant of marriage,
do you affirm your desire and intention to enter this
covenant?

The man answers:

I do.

The minister addresses the bride:

_____, having heard how God honors the
covenant of marriage,
do you affirm your desire and intention to enter this
covenant?

The woman answers:

I do.

Selection D

The minister addresses the groom:

_____, in your baptism
you have been called to union with Christ and the
church.
Do you intend to honor this calling
through the covenant of marriage?

Answer:

I do.

The minister addresses the bride:

_____, in your baptism
you have been called to union with Christ and the
church.
Do you intend to honor this calling
through the covenant of marriage?

Answer:

I do.

Selection E

Then shall the minister say to the man:

_____, will you have this woman to be
your wedded wife, to live together after God's ordinance in the holy estate of matrimony? Will you
love her, comfort her, honor and keep her in sickness and in health, and, forsaking all others, remain
faithful to her, so long as you both shall live?

The man shall say:

I will.

Then shall the minister say to the woman:

_____, will you have this man to be your
wedded husband, to live together after God's ordinance in the holy estate of matrimony? Will you
love him, comfort him, honor and keep him in sickness and in health, and, forsaking all others, remain
faithful to him, so long as you both shall live?

The woman shall say:

I will.

Selection F

Then shall the minister say to the man:

_____, will you have this woman to be
your wedded wife, to live together in God's grace in
the holy relationship of marriage? Will you love her,
comfort her, honor and keep her in sickness and in
health, and, forsaking all others, remain faithful to
her, so long as you both shall live?

The man shall say:

I will.

Then shall the minister say to the woman:

_____, will you have this man to be your
wedded husband, to live together in God's grace in
the holy relationship of marriage? Will you love him,
comfort him, honor and keep him in sickness and in
health, and, forsaking all others, remain faithful to
him, so long as you both shall live?

The woman shall say:

I will.

Selection G

Then shall the minister say to the man, using his Christian name:

_____, will you have this woman to be your wedded wife, to live together in the holy estate of matrimony? Will you love her, comfort her, honor and keep her, in sickness and in health; and forsaking all others remain loyal to her as long as you both shall live?

The man shall answer:

I will.

Then shall the minister say to the woman, using her Christian name:

_____, will you have this man to be your wedded husband, to live together in the holy estate of matrimony? Will you love him, comfort him, honor and keep him, in sickness and in health; and forsaking all others remain loyal to him as long as you both shall live?

The woman shall answer:

I will.

Selection H

The minister shall say to the man, addressing him by his Christian name:

_____, will you have this woman to be your wife, to live together in the holy bond of marriage? Will you love her, honor her, and care for her, under all conditions and circumstances of life, and through the grace of God approve yourself a faithful Christian husband to her so long as you both shall live? If this is your desire then answer and say, "I will."

The man shall answer:

I will.

The minister shall say to the woman, addressing her by her Christian name:

_____, will you have this man to be your husband, to live together in the holy bond of marriage? Will you love him, honor him, and care for him, under all conditions and circumstances of life, and through the grace of God approve yourself a faithful Christian wife to him so long as you both shall live? If this is your desire then answer and say, "I will."

The woman shall answer:

I will.

Selection I

The minister shall say to the man, addressing him by his Christian name:

_____, will you have this woman to be your wife, to live together in the holy bond of marriage? Will you love her, honor her, and care for her, under all conditions and circumstances of life, and through the grace of God be a faithful Christian husband to her so long as you both shall live? If this is your desire then answer and say, "I will."

The man shall answer:

I will.

The minister shall say to the woman, addressing her by her Christian name:

_____, will you have this man to be your husband, to live together in the holy bond of marriage? Will you love him, honor him, and care for him, under all conditions and circumstances of life, and through the grace of God be a faithful Christian wife to him so long as you both shall live? If this is your desire then answer and say, "I will."

The woman shall answer:

I will.

Selection J

The minister shall say to the man:

_____, will you have this woman to be your wife, and be faithful to her alone?

The man shall answer:

I will, with the help of God.

The minister shall say to the woman:

_____, will you have this man to be your husband, and be faithful to him alone?

The woman shall answer:

I will, with the help of God.

Selection K

Then the minister says to the man:

_____, will you have this woman,
_____, to be your wife,
and cleave to her alone?

And the man answers:

I will.

The minister says to the woman:

_____, will you have this man,
_____, to be your husband,
and cleave to him alone?

And the woman answers:

I will.

Selection L

Then the minister says to the man:

_____, will you have this woman,
_____, to be your wife,
and be faithful to her alone?

And the man answers:

I will.

The minister says to the woman:

_____, will you have this man,
_____, to be your husband,
and be faithful to him alone?

And the woman answers:

I will.

Selection M

The minister addresses the couple:

Before God and this congregation,
I ask you to affirm your willingness
to enter this covenant of marriage
and to share all the joys and sorrows
of this new relationship,
whatever the future may hold.

The minister addresses the groom:

_____,

will you have _____ to be your wife,
and will you love her faithfully
as long as you both shall live?

Groom:

I will, with the help of God.

The minister addresses the bride:

_____,

will you have _____ to be your husband,
and will you love him faithfully,
as long as you both shall live?

Bride:

I will, with the help of God.

Selection N

The minister says to the woman:

_____, will you have this man to be your husband; to live together in the covenant of marriage? Will you love him, comfort him, honor and keep him, in sickness and in health; and, forsaking all others, be faithful to him as long as you both shall live?

The woman answers:

I will.

The minister says to the man:

_____, will you have this woman to be your wife; to live together in the covenant of marriage? Will you love her, comfort her, honor and keep her, in sickness and in health; and, forsaking all others, be faithful to her as long as you both shall live?

The man answers:

I will.

Selection O

Speaking to the groom, the minister will say:

_____, do you take _____ to be your wife, and do you commit yourself to her, to be responsible in the marriage relationship, to give yourself to her in love and work, to invite her fully into your being so that she can know who you are, to cherish her above all others and to respect her individuality, encouraging her to be herself and to grow in all that God intends?

The groom will answer:

Yes, I do.

Speaking to the bride, the minister will say:

_____, do you take _____ to be your husband, and do you commit yourself to him, to be responsible in the marriage relationship, to give yourself to him in love and work, to invite him fully into your being so that he can know who you are, to cherish him above all others and to respect his individuality, encouraging him to be himself and to grow in all that God intends?

The bride will answer:

Yes, I do.

Selection P

Minister to the persons who are to marry:

I ask you now
in the presence of God and these people
to declare your intention
to enter into union with one another
through the grace of Jesus Christ,
who has called you into union with himself
through baptism.

Minister to the woman:

_____, will you have _____
   to be your husband,
to live together in holy marriage?
Will you love him, comfort him, honor and keep him
in sickness and in health,
and forsaking all others, be faithful to him
as long as you both shall live?

Woman:

I will.

Minister to the man:

_____, will you have _____
   to be your wife,
to live together in holy marriage?
Will you love her, comfort her, honor and keep her
in sickness and in health,
and forsaking all others, be faithful to her
as long as you both shall live?

Man:

I will.

Selection Q

The persons to be married shall stand with their attendants before the minister, who shall ask the man:

_____, will you receive _____
as your wife and bind yourself to her in the covenant of marriage? Will you promise to love and honor her in true devotion; to rejoice with her in time of felicity and grieve with her in times of sorrow; and be faithful to her as long as you both shall live?

Man:

I will, with the help of God.

The minister shall ask the woman:

_____, will you receive _____ as your husband and bind yourself to him in the covenant of marriage? Will you promise to love and honor him in true devotion; to rejoice with him in times of felicity and grieve with him in times of sorrow; and be faithful to him as long as you both shall live?

Woman:

I will, with the help of God.

Selection R

Then the minister may ask them:

_____ and _____, do you believe that God has blessed and guided you, and now calls you into marriage?

The bridegroom and bride each answer:

I do.

The minister shall ask the bridegroom:

_____, will you give yourself to _____ to be her husband, to live together in the covenant of marriage? Will you love her, comfort her, honor and protect her, and, forsaking all others, be faithful to her as long as you both shall live?

He answers:

I will.

The minister shall ask the bride:

_____, will you give yourself to _____ to be his wife, to live together in the covenant of marriage? Will you love him, comfort him, honor and protect him, and, forsaking all others, be faithful to him, as long as you both shall live?

She answers:

I will.

Category 5:
Leavetaking

Selection A

The minister shall ask the family members of the persons to be married:

Will you receive _____ and _____ into your family and uphold them with your love as they establish themselves as a family within your own?

Representatives from both families answer:

We will.

Selection B

The minister shall ask the family members of the persons to be married:

Will you receive _____ and _____ into your family and uphold them with your love as they establish themselves as a family within your own?

Representatives from both families answer:

We will.

The minister addresses the congregation and may ask them to stand:

Will you witness this covenant between _____ and _____, respect their marriage, and sustain them with your friendship and care? If so, please say, "We will."

Congregation:

We will.

Selection C

Pastor, addressing each child by name:

_____,
you are entering a new family.
Will you give to this new family
your trust, love, and affection?

Each child:

I will, with the help of God.

Pastor, addressing the bride and groom:

_____ and _____,
will you be faithful and loving parents
to _____?

Couple:

We will, with the help of God.

•

The pastor may invite the immediate families of the groom and bride, including adults or young children from previous relationships, to stand in place, if they are able, and to offer their support in these or similar words.

Pastor, addressing the families:

Will the families of _____ and

_____
(please stand/please answer) in support of this
 couple.
Do you offer your prayerful blessing
and loving support to this marriage?
If so, please say, "I do."

Family members:

I do.

> *All family members may be seated. The person(s) who
> escorted the bride may be seated with her family.*

> *The pastor may address the congregation in these or
> similar words.*

Pastor, addressing the congregation:

Do you, as people of God,
pledge your support and encouragement
to the covenant commitment that
_____ and _____ are making
 together?
If so, please say, "We do."

People:

We do.

Selection D

> *At this point the minister may ask:*

Who presents this woman to be married to this man?

> *The father, or representative of the family, may respond:*

I do.

Selection E

> *At this point the minister may ask:*

Who presents this woman to be married to this man?

> *The father, or representative of the family, may respond:*

Her mother and I.

Selection F

> *At this point the minister may ask:*

Who presents this woman to be married to this man?

> *The father, or representative of the family, may respond:*

Her family and I.

Selection G

> *The minister may address the families of the bride and
> groom:*

(name of family members) _____,
do you give your blessing to _____ and
_____,
and promise to do everything in your power to
 uphold them in their marriage?

> *Answer:*

We give our blessing
and promise our loving support.

> *The families may be seated.*

> *The minister may then address the congregation. The
> congregation may stand.*

Will all of you witnessing these vows
do everything in your power to uphold
_____ and _____
in their marriage?

> *Answer:*

We will.

Selection H

> *The minister may address the families of the bride and
> groom:*

(name of family members) _____,
do you give your blessing to _____ and
_____,
and promise to do everything in your power to
 uphold them in their marriage?

Answer:

We give our blessing
and promise our loving support.

> *The families may be seated.*

Selection I

> *The minister may address the families of the bride and groom:*

(name of family members) _____,
do you give your blessing to _____ and
_____,
and promise to do everything in your power to
uphold them in their marriage?

> *Answer:*

We do.

> *The families may be seated.*

> *The minister may then address the congregation. The congregation may stand.*

Will all of you witnessing these vows
do everything in your power to uphold
_____ and _____
in their marriage?

> *Answer:*

We will.

Selection J

> *The minister may address the families of the bride and groom:*

(name of family members) _____,
do you give your blessing to _____ and
_____,
and promise to do everything in your power to
uphold them in their marriage?

> *Answer:*

We do.

> *The families may be seated.*

Selection K

> *The minister may address the families of the bride and groom:*

(name of family members) _____,
do you give your blessing to _____ and
_____,
and promise to do everything in your power to
uphold them in their marriage?

> *Answer:*

I give my blessing
and promise my loving support.

> *The families may be seated.*

> *The minister may then address the congregation. The congregation may stand.*

Will all of you witnessing these vows
do everything in your power to uphold
_____ and _____
in their marriage?

> *Answer:*

We will.

Selection L

> *The minister may address the families of the bride and groom:*

(name of family members) _____,
do you give your blessing to _____ and
_____,
and promise to do everything in your power to
uphold them in their marriage?

> *Answer:*

I give my blessing
and promise my loving support.

> *The families may be seated.*

Selection M

The minister may address the families of the bride and groom:

(name of family members) _____,
do you give your blessing to _____ and

_____,

and promise to do everything in your power to uphold them in their marriage?

> *Answer:*

I do.

> *The families may be seated.*

> *The minister may then address the congregation. The congregation may stand.*

Will all of you witnessing these vows
do everything in your power to uphold
_____ and _____
in their marriage?

> *Answer:*

We will.

Selection N

The minister may address the families of the bride and groom:

(name of family members) _____,
do you give your blessing to _____ and

_____,

and promise to do everything in your power to uphold them in their marriage?

> *Answer:*

I do.

> *The families may be seated.*

Selection O

If the woman is presented or given in marriage, the minister shall now receive her at the hands of her father, or representative of the family, the woman placing her right hand in the hand of the minister. Then shall
the minister place the right hand of the woman in the right hand of the man.

No questions are asked of the bride's family.

Selection P

If the woman be given in marriage, the minister shall say:

Who gives this woman to be married to this man?

> *No verbal response is given by the bride's family. Instead, the minister shall then receive her at the hands of her father, friend, or representative of the family, the woman placing her right hand in the hand of the minister. Then shall the minister place the right hand of the woman in the right hand of the man.*

Selection Q

If the woman be presented in marriage, the minister shall say:

Who presents this woman to be married to this man?

> *No verbal response is given by the bride's family. Instead, the minister shall then receive her at the hands of her father, friend, or representative of the family, the woman placing her right hand in the hand of the minister. Then shall the minister place the right hand of the woman in the right hand of the man.*

Selection R

If the father, or representative of the family, is not present, the minister may say:

_____ and _____, give each other the right hand.

Selection S

The minister says:

Who presents this woman and this man to be married to each other?

> *The father, or representative of the bride's family, says:*

I do.

The best man, or representative of the groom's family, says:

I do.

Selection T

The minister says:

Who presents this woman and this man to be married to each other?

The father, or representative of the bride's family, says:

On behalf of the family, I do.

The best man, or representative of the groom's family, says:

On behalf of the family, I do.

Selection U

Inviting the parents to stand, the minister shall ask:

Do you as parents promise to pray for and support your children in this new relationship which they enter as husband and wife? If so, each say "I do."

The parents say:

I do.

Addressing the congregation, the minister shall say:

All of you who witness these vows, will you do everything in your power to support and uphold these two persons in their marriage? Then say, "We will!"

Selection V

The minister asks the families of the bride and bridegroom:

Do you the families of _____ and _____ promise to pray for and support this new relationship which they enter as husband and wife?

A representative of each family (i.e., best man or father and presenter of the bride or maid/matron of honor) shall answer:

We do.

Selection W

The minister says:

The marriage of _____ and _____ unites two families and creates a new one. They ask your blessing.

Parents or other representatives of the families, if present, may respond:

We rejoice in your union,
and pray God's blessing upon you.

Minister to people:

Will all of you, by God's grace,
do everything in your power
to uphold and care for these two persons
in their marriage?

People:

We will.

Selection X

The minister says:

The marriage of
_____ and _____
unites two families
and creates a new one.
They ask for your blessing.

The minister addresses the family representatives:

Do you give your blessing to this marriage?

Family representatives respond:

We do.

Selection Y

The minister says:

The marriage of
_____ and _____
unites two families
and creates a new one.
They ask for your blessing.

The minister addresses the family representatives:

Do you give your blessing to this marriage and do you promise to do everything in your power to uphold and care for these two persons in their marriage?

Family representatives respond:

We do.

Selection Z

At this point the minister may ask:

Who gives this woman to be married to this man?

The father, or representative of the family, may respond:

I do.

Selection AA

At this point the minister may ask:

Who gives this woman to be married to this man?

The father, or representative of the family, may respond:

Her mother and I.

Selection BB

At this point the minister may ask:

Who gives this woman to be married to this man?

The father, or representative of the family, may respond:

Her family and I.

Selection CC

The minister asks the parents of the bride and bridegroom:

Do you, the parents of
_____ and _____,
give your blessing to their marriage?

The parents of the bride and bridegroom say:

We do.

Selection DD

The minister asks the families of the bride and bridegroom:

Do you, on behalf of your family,
give your blessing to this marriage?

A member of each family says:

I do.

Selection EE

The minister asks the family of either the bride or bridegroom:

Do you, on behalf of both families,
give your blessing to this marriage?

A member of one family says:

I do.

Category 6:
The Vows

Selection A

*The bride and groom join hands and face each other.
The man says:*

I, _____, take you, _____, to be my wedded wife, to have and to hold, from this day forward, for better, for worse, for richer, for poorer, in sickness and in health, to love and to cherish, till death us do part, according to God's holy ordinance; and thereto I pledge myself truly with all my heart.

The woman says:

I, _____, take you, _____, as my wedded husband, to have and to hold, from this day forward, for better, for worse, for richer, for poorer, in sickness and in health, to love and to cherish, till death us do part, according to God's holy ordinance; and thereto I pledge myself truly with all my heart.

Selection B

*The bride and groom join hands and face each other.
The man says:*

I, _____, take you, _____, to be my wedded wife, to have and to hold, from this day forward, for better, for worse, for richer, for poorer, in sickness and in health, to love and to cherish, till death us do part, according to God's holy ordi-

nance; and to you I pledge myself truly with all my heart.

The woman says:

I, _____, take you, _____, as my wedded husband, to have and to hold, from this day forward, for better, for worse, for richer, for poorer, in sickness and in health, to love and to cherish, till death us do part, according to God's holy ordinance; and to you I pledge myself truly with all my heart.

Selection C

*The bride and groom join hands and face each other.
The man says:*

I, _____, take you, _____, to be my wedded wife; and I do promise and covenant; before God and these witnesses; to be your loving and faithful husband; in plenty and in want; in joy and in sorrow; in sickness and in health; as long as we both shall live.

The woman says:

I, _____, take you, _____, to be my wedded husband; and I do promise and covenant; before God and these witnesses; to be your loving and faithful wife; in plenty and in want; in joy and in sorrow; in sickness and in health; as long as we both shall live.

Selection D

The minister addresses the couple:

_____ and _____,
since it is your intention to marry,
join your right hands,
and with your promises
bind yourselves to each other as husband and wife.

> *The bride and groom face each other and join right hands. Then, they shall say their vows to each other, in turn.*

> *The man says:*

I, _____, take you, _____,
    to be my wife;
and I promise,
before God and these witnesses,
to be your loving and faithful husband;
in plenty and in want;
in joy and in sorrow;
in sickness and in health;
as long as we both shall live.

> *The woman says:*

I, _____, take you, _____,
    to be my husband;
and I promise,
before God and these witnesses,
to be your loving and faithful wife;
in plenty and in want;
in joy and in sorrow;
in sickness and in health;
as long as we both shall live.

Selection E

The minister addresses the couple:

_____ and _____,
since it is your intention to marry,
join your right hands,
and with your promises
bind yourselves to each other as husband and wife.

> *The bride and groom face each other and join right hands. Then, they shall say their vows to each other, in turn.*

> *The man says:*

Before God and these witnesses,
I, _____, take you, _____,
to be my wife,
and I promise to love you,
and to be faithful to you
as long as we both shall live.

> *The woman says:*

Before God and these witnesses,
I, _____, take you, _____,
to be my husband,
and I promise to love you,
and to be faithful to you
as long as we both shall live.

Selection F

> *The bride and groom join hands and face each other. The man says:*

I, _____, take you, _____, to be my wedded wife, and I pledge you my faithfulness, till death us do part.

> *The woman says:*

I, _____, take you, _____, to be my wedded husband, and I pledge you my faithfulness, till death us do part.

Selection G

> *The minister says:*

_____ and _____, you have come together according to God's wonderful plan for creation. Now, before these people say your vows to each other.

> *The bride and groom join hands and face each other.*

> *The minister says:*

Be subject to one another out of reverence for Christ.

The man shall say to the woman:

_____, I promise with God's help to be your faithful husband, to love and serve you as Christ commands, as long as we both shall live.

The woman shall say to the man:

_____, I promise with God's help to be your faithful wife, to love and serve you as Christ commands, as long as we both shall live.

Selection H

The bride and groom join hands and face each other. The man says:

_____, I promise with God's help to be your faithful husband, to love and serve you as Christ commands, as long as we both shall live.

The woman shall say to the man:

_____, I promise with God's help to be your faithful wife, to love and serve you as Christ commands, as long as we both shall live.

Selection I

The bride and groom join hands and face each other. The man says:

I, _____, take thee, _____, to be my wedded wife, to have and to hold, from this day forward, for better, for worse, for richer, for poorer, in sickness and in health, to love and to cherish, till death us do part, according to God's holy ordinance; and thereto I pledge thee my faith.

The woman says:

I, _____, take thee, _____, to be my wedded husband, to have and to hold, from this day forward, for better, for worse, for richer, for poorer, in sickness and in health, to love and to cherish, till death us do part, according to God's holy ordinance; and thereto I pledge thee my faith.

Selection J

The bride and groom join hands and face each other. The man says:

I, _____, take you, _____, to be my wedded wife, to have and to hold, from this day forward, for better, for worse, for richer, for poorer, in sickness and in health, to love and to cherish, till death us do part, according to God's holy ordinance; and to you I pledge my faith.

The woman says:

I, _____, take you, _____, to be my wedded husband, to have and to hold, from this day forward, for better, for worse, for richer, for poorer, in sickness and in health, to love and to cherish, till death us do part, according to God's holy ordinance; and to you I pledge my faith.

Selection K

The bride and groom join hands and face each other. The man says:

I take you, _____,
to be my wife from this day forward,
to join with you and share all that is to come,
and I promise to be faithful to you
until death parts us.

The woman says:

I take you, _____,
to be my husband from this day forward,
to join with you and share all that is to come,
and I promise to be faithful to you
until death parts us.

Selection L

The bride and groom join hands and face each other. The man says:

I, _____, take you, _____, to be my wedded wife, and I pledge my faithfulness to you, till death shall part us.

The woman says:

I, _____, take you, _____, to be my wedded husband, and I pledge my faithfulness to you, till death shall part us.

Selection M

The bride and groom join hands and face each other. The man says:

I, _____, take you, _____, to be my wedded wife; and I do promise and covenant to be your loving and faithful husband; for better, for worse; for richer, for poorer; in sickness and in health; so long as we both shall live.

The woman says:

I, _____, take you, _____, to be my wedded husband; and I do promise and covenant to be your loving and faithful wife; for better, for worse; for richer, for poorer; in sickness and in health; so long as we both shall live.

Selection N

The bride and groom join hands and face each other. The man says:

I, _____, take you, _____, to be my wife, and I promise to love and sustain you in the bonds of marriage from this day forward, in sickness and in health, in plenty and in want, in joy and in sorrow, till death shall part us, according to God's holy ordinance.

The woman says:

I, _____, take you, _____, to be my husband, and I promise to love and sustain you in the bonds of marriage from this day forward, in sickness and in health, in plenty and in want, in joy and in sorrow, till death shall part us, according to God's holy ordinance.

Selection O

Then the minister shall say to the bride and groom:

As a seal to the vows you are about to make, give each other the right hand.

Then they shall say after the minister:

I, _____, now take you, _____, to be my wife. In the presence of God and before these witnesses I promise to be a loving, faithful, and loyal husband to you, until God shall separate us by death.

I, _____, now take you, _____, to be my husband. In the presence of God and before these witnesses I promise to be a loving, faithful, and loyal wife to you, until God shall separate us by death.

Selection P

Then the minister shall say to the bride and groom:

Do you, _____, now take _____ to be your wife; and do you promise, in the presence of God and before these witnesses, to be a loving, faithful, and loyal husband to her, until God shall separate you by death?

Answer:

I do.

Do you, _____, now take _____ to be your husband; and do you promise, in the presence of God and before these witnesses, to be a loving, faithful, and loyal wife to him, until God shall separate you by death?

Answer:

I do.

Selection Q

The bride and groom join hands and face each other. The man says:

I, _____, take you, _____, to be my wife, to have and to hold from this day forward;

for better, for worse; for richer, for poorer; in sickness and in health; to love, cherish, and honor, till death us do part, according to God's holy law; and to this I give you my pledge.

The woman says:

I, _____, take you, _____, to be my husband, to have and to hold from this day forward; for better, for worse; for richer, for poorer; in sickness and in health; to love, cherish, and honor, till death us do part, according to God's holy law; and to this I give you my pledge.

The minister says:

God has heard your vows, and we are witnesses.

Selection R

The bride and groom join hands and face each other. The man says:

In the Name of God, I, _____, take you, _____, to be my wife, to have and to hold from this day forward, for better for worse, for richer for poorer, in sickness and in health, to love and to cherish, until we are parted by death. This is my solemn vow.

The woman says:

In the Name of God, I, _____, take you, _____, to be my husband, to have and to hold from this day forward, for better for worse, for richer for poorer, in sickness and in health, to love and to cherish, until we are parted by death. This is my solemn vow.

Selection S

The bridegroom turns and faces the people, and says:

I ask everyone here to witness
that I, _____, take _____
    to be my wife,
according to God's holy will.

He then faces the bride, takes her hands, and says:

_____,
all that I am I give to you,

and all that I have I share with you.
Whatever the future holds,
I will love you and stand by you,
as long as we both shall live.
This is my solemn vow.

They loose hands.

The bride turns and faces the people, and says:

I ask everyone here to witness
that I, _____, take _____
    to be my husband,
according to God's holy will.

She then faces the bridegroom, takes his hands, and says:

_____,
all that I am I give to you,
and all that I have I share with you.
Whatever the future holds,
I will love you and stand by you,
as long as we both shall live.
This is my solemn vow.

They loose hands.

Selection T

The bride and groom join hands and face each other. The man says:

I take you, _____, to be my wife from this day forward, to join with you and share all that is to come; and, with the help of God, I promise to be faithful to you as God gives us life together.

The woman says:

I take you, _____, to be my husband from this day forward, to join with you and share all that is to come; and, with the help of God, I promise to be faithful to you as God gives us life together.

Selection U

The bride and groom join hands and face each other. The man says:

Before God and these witnesses, and in reliance upon the grace of our Lord Jesus Christ, I,

_____, take you, _____, to be my wife,

> to have and to hold
> to love and to cherish
> to give and to receive
> to speak and to listen
> to confront and to comfort
> to repent and to forgive
> to encourage and to respond
> to respect and honor

"for where you go, I will go; your people will be my people; and your God will be my God." I promise to bear with you and to be faithful to you in all circumstances of our life together so that we may join to serve God and others as long as we both shall live.

The woman says:

Before God and these witnesses, and in reliance upon the grace of our Lord Jesus Christ, I, _____, take you, _____, to be my husband,

> to have and to hold
> to love and to cherish
> to give and to receive
> to speak and to listen
> to confront and to comfort
> to repent and to forgive
> to encourage and to respond
> to respect and honor

"for where you go, I will go; your people will be my people; and your God will be my God." I promise to bear with you and to be faithful to you in all circumstances of our life together so that we may join to serve God and others as long as we both shall live.

Selection V

The bride and groom join hands and face each other. The man says:

I take you, _____, to be my wife. I promise before God and these witnesses to be your faithful husband, to share with you in plenty and in want, in joy and in sorrow, in sickness and in health, to forgive and strengthen you and to join with you so that together we may serve God and others so long as we both shall live.

The woman says:

I take you, _____, to be my husband. I promise before God and these witnesses to be your faithful wife, to share with you in plenty and in want, in joy and in sorrow, in sickness and in health, to forgive and strengthen you and to join with you so that together we may serve God and others as long as we both shall live.

Selection W

The woman and man face each other, joining hands. The man says:

In the name of God,
I, _____, take you, _____,
to be my wife,
to have and to hold
from this day forward,
for better for worse,
for richer for poorer,
in sickness and in health,
to love and to cherish,
until we are parted by death.
This is my solemn vow.

The woman says:

In the name of God,
I, _____, take you, _____,
to be my husband,
to have and to hold
from this day forward,
for better for worse,
for richer for poorer,
in sickness and in health,
to love and to cherish,
until we are parted by death.
This is my solemn vow.

Selection X

The minister shall say to the man and the woman:

_____ and _____, before God and these witnesses, make your covenant of marriage with each other.

The man shall face the woman, take her hand in his and say:

I, _____, take you, _____,
   to be my wife,
to have and to hold from this day forward,
for better, for worse,
for richer, for poorer,
in sickness and in health,
to love and to cherish
as long as we both shall live.
To this I pledge myself
truly with all my heart.

The woman, still facing the man and taking his hand in hers, shall say:

I, _____, take you, _____,
   to be my husband,
to have and to hold from this day forward,
for better, for worse,
for richer, for poorer,
in sickness and in health,
to love and to cherish
as long as we both shall live.
To this I pledge myself
truly with all my heart.

Selection Y

The man and the woman shall face each other and take hands. They shall say to each other, in turn:

_____,
I give myself to you in marriage
and vow to be your (husband/wife)
all the days of our lives.

I give you my hands
and take your hands in mine
as a symbol and pledge
of our uniting in one flesh.

I give you my love,
the outpouring of my heart,
as a symbol and pledge
of our uniting in one spirit.

Selection Z

The minister may introduce the covenant promises in the following or similar words.

_____ and _____, by your covenant promises shared with us, unite yourselves in marriage and be subject to one another out of reverence for Christ.

or

_____ and _____, speak your covenant promises that you have come to offer before God.

The couple may face each other and join hands, the women first giving her bouquet, if any, to an attendant. The groom and bride say:

BRIDE:

_____,
I give myself to you to be your wife.
I promise to love and sustain you
in the covenant of marriage,
from this day forward,
in sickness and in health,
in plenty and in want,
in joy and in sorrow,
as long as we both shall live.

GROOM:

_____,
I give myself to you to be your husband.
I promise to love and sustain you
in the covenant of marriage,
from this day forward,
in sickness and in health,
in plenty and in want,
in joy and in sorrow,
as long as we both shall live.

Selection AA

The bride and bridegroom face each other and join hands.

The bridegroom says:

I, _____, in the presence of God,
take you, _____, to be my wife;

to have and to hold
from this day forward,
for better, for worse,
for richer, for poorer,
in sickness and in health,
to love and to cherish,
as long as we both shall live.
This is my solemn vow.

The bride says:

I, _____, in the presence of God,
take you, _____, to be my husband;
to have and to hold
from this day forward,
for better, for worse,
for richer, for poorer,
in sickness and in health,
to love and to cherish,
as long as we both shall live.
This is my solemn vow.

They loose hands.

Selection BB

The bride and bridegroom face each other and join hands.

The bridegroom says:

I, _____, take you, _____,
to be my wife,
according to God's holy will.
I will love you,
and share my life with you,
in sickness and in health,
in poverty and in prosperity,
in conflict and in harmony,
as long as we both shall live.
This is my solemn vow.

The bride says:

I, _____, take you, _____,
to be my husband,
according to God's holy will.
I will love you,
and share my life with you,
in sickness and in health,
in poverty and in prosperity,
in conflict and in harmony,
as long as we both shall live.
This is my solemn vow.

They loose hands.

Selection CC

The bride and bridegroom face each other and join hands.

The bridegroom says:

I, _____, in the presence of God,
take you, _____, to be my wife.
All that I am I give to you,
and all that I have I share with you.
Whatever the future holds,
I will love you and stand by you,
as long as we both shall live.
This is my solemn vow.

The bride says:

I, _____, in the presence of God,
take you, _____, to be my husband.
All that I am I give to you,
and all that I have I share with you.
Whatever the future holds,
I will love you and stand by you,
as long as we both shall live.
This is my solemn vow.

They loose hands.

Category 7:
Exchange of Rings

Selection A

The minister says:

What token do you give of this your marriage vow?

The man, placing the ring on the woman's hand, shall say:

This ring I give in token of the covenant made this day between us; in the name of the Father and of the Son and of the Holy Spirit. Amen.

The woman, placing the ring on the man's hand, shall say:

This ring I give in token of the covenant made this day between us; in the name of the Father and of the Son and of the Holy Spirit. Amen.

Selection B

The minister says:

What token do you give of this your marriage vow?

The man, placing the ring on the woman's hand, shall say:

With this ring, I thee wed; in the name of the Father and of the Son and of the Holy Spirit. Amen.

The woman, placing the ring on the man's hand, shall say:

With this ring, I thee wed; in the name of the Father and of the Son and of the Holy Spirit. Amen.

Selection C

If rings be provided, one shall be given to the minister, who shall return it to the man, who shall then put it upon the woman's ring finger, saying after the minister:

This ring I give you; in token and pledge of our constant faith; and abiding love.

The woman, receiving the other ring from the minister, shall then put it upon the man's ring finger, saying after the minister:

This ring I give you; in token and pledge of our constant faith; and abiding love.

Selection D

Before giving the ring the minister may say:

Bless, O Lord, the covenant these rings symbolize, that they who give and wear them may remain in your peace, and continue in your favor, until their life's end; through Jesus Christ our Lord. Amen.

The man, placing the ring on the hand of the woman, says:

This ring I give you; in token and pledge of our constant faith; and abiding love.

The woman, placing the ring on the hand of the man, says:

This ring I give you; in token and pledge of our constant faith; and abiding love.

Selection E

Pastor:

_____ and _____,
what will you share to symbolize your love?

> *The groom and bride may name the symbol(s) and present them/it to the pastor, who may hold or place a hand on the symbol(s) and offer one of these or another prayer.*

Let us pray.
Eternal God, who in the time of Noah, gave us the rainbow as a sign of promise, bless (these symbols/this symbol) that (they/it) also may be (signs/a sign) of promises fulfilled in lives of faithful loving; through Jesus Christ our Savior. Amen.

> *Groom:*

_____,
I give you (this/these) _____
as a sign of my love and faithfulness.

> *Bride:*

I receive (this/these) _____
as a sign of our love and faithfulness.

> *Bride:*

_____,
I give you (this/these) _____
as a sign of my love and faithfulness.

> *Groom:*

I receive (this/these) _____
as a sign of our love and faithfulness.

Selection F

> *If rings are to be exchanged, the minister says to the couple:*

What do you bring as a sign of your promise?

> *When the rings are presented the minister may say the following prayer:*

By your blessing, O God,
may these rings be to
_____ and _____

symbols of unending love and faithfulness,
reminding them of the covenant they have made this
  day,
through Jesus Christ our Lord. Amen.

> *The bride and groom shall exchange rings using these or other appropriate words.*

> *The one giving the ring says:*

_____, I give you this ring
as a sign of our covenant,
in the name of the Father,
and of the Son,
and of the Holy Spirit.

> *The one receiving the ring says:*

I receive this ring,
as a sign of our covenant
in the name of the Father,
and of the Son,
and of the Holy Spirit.

Selection G

> *If rings are to be exchanged, the minister says to the couple:*

What do you bring as a sign of your promise?

> *When the rings are presented the minister may say the following prayer:*

By your blessing, O God,
may these rings be to
_____ and _____
symbols of unending love and faithfulness,
reminding them of the covenant they have made this
  day,
through Jesus Christ our Lord.

Amen.

> *The bride and groom shall exchange rings using these or other appropriate words.*

> *As each ring is given, the one giving the ring says:*

This ring I give you,
as a sign of our constant faith
and abiding love,

in the name of the Father,
and of the Son,
and of the Holy Spirit.

The one receiving the ring says:

I receive this ring,
as a sign of our covenant
in the name of the Father,
and of the Son,
and of the Holy Spirit.

Selection H

The man receives the ring from the minister and places it on the hand of the woman, saying:

Receive this ring as a token of my love and faithfulness.

The woman receives the ring from the minister and places it on the hand of the man, saying:

Receive this ring as a token of my love and faithfulness.

Selection I

The man receives the ring from the minister and places it on the hand of the woman, saying:

_____, receive this ring as a token of my love and faithfulness.

The woman receives the ring from the minister and places it on the hand of the man, saying:

_____, receive this ring as a token of my love and faithfulness.

Selection J

The man receives the ring from the minister and places it on the hand of the woman, saying:

I give you this ring as a sign of my promise.

The woman receives the ring from the minister and places it on the hand of the man, saying:

I give you this ring as a sign of my promise.

Selection K

The minister taking the rings shall say:

The wedding ring is the outward and visible sign of an inward and spiritual grace, signifying to all the uniting of this man and this woman in holy marriage, through the church of Jesus Christ our Lord.

Then the minister says:

Let us pray.
Bless, O Lord, the giving of these rings, that they who wear them may abide in your peace, and continue in your favor: through Jesus Christ our Lord. Amen.

The minister shall then deliver the proper ring to the man to put upon the woman's ring finger. The man, holding the ring there, shall say after the minister:

In token and pledge of our constant faith and abiding love, with this ring, I thee wed, in the name of the Father, and of the Son, and of the Holy Spirit. Amen.

Then the minister shall deliver the second ring to the woman to put upon the man's ring finger; and the woman, holding the ring there, shall say after the minister:

In token and pledge of our constant faith and abiding love, with this ring I thee wed, in the name of the Father, and of the Son, and of the Holy Spirit. Amen.

Selection L

The minister shall receive the first ring and give it to the man to place on the woman's left hand.

The man shall say:

This ring I give you in token of my faithfulness and love, and as a pledge to honor you with my whole being, and to share with you my worldly goods.

The minister shall receive the other ring and then give it to the woman to place on the man's left hand.

The woman shall say:

This ring I give you in token of my faithfulness and love, and as a pledge to honor you with my whole being, and to share with you my worldly goods.

Selection M

When only one ring is given, the minister shall receive the ring and give it to the man to place on the woman's left hand.

The man shall say:

This ring I give you in token of my faithfulness and love, and as a pledge to honor you with my whole being, and to share with you my worldly goods.

The woman shall say:

This ring I receive in token of my faithfulness and love, and as a pledge to honor you with my whole being, and to share with you my worldly goods.

Selection N

The rings shall be given to the minister, who shall return them saying:

As a token of the covenant into which you have entered, these rings are given and received.

Selection O

The man, receiving the ring from the minister, puts it on the woman's finger and says after the minister:

This ring I give you in token of constant faith and abiding love. I honor you with my body, and all my worldly goods with you I share.

The woman, receiving the ring from the minister, puts it on the man's finger and says after the minister:

This ring I give you in token of constant faith and abiding love. I honor you with my body, and all my worldly goods with you I share.

Selection P

The minister may ask God's blessing on the rings as follows:

Bless, O Lord, these rings to be a sign of the vows by which this man and this woman have bound themselves to each other; through Jesus Christ our Lord. Amen.

The man places the ring on the ring finger of the other's hand and says:

_____, I give you this ring as a symbol of my vow, and with all that I am, and all that I have, I honor you, in the Name of the Father, and of the Son, and of the Holy Spirit.

The woman places the ring on the ring finger of the other's hand and says:

_____, I give you this ring as a symbol of my vow, and with all that I am, and all that I have, I honor you, in the Name of the Father, and of the Son, and of the Holy Spirit.

Selection Q

The minister may ask God's blessing on the rings as follows:

Bless, O Lord, these rings to be a sign of the vows by which this man and this woman have bound themselves to each other; through Jesus Christ our Lord. Amen.

The man places the ring on the ring finger of the other's hand and says:

_____, I give you this ring as a symbol of my vow, and with all that I am, and all that I have, I honor you, in the Name of God.

The woman places the ring on the ring finger of the other's hand and says:

_____, I give you this ring as a symbol of my vow, and with all that I am, and all that I have, I honor you, in the Name of God.

Selection R

As the minister receives each ring in turn, it is appropriate to pray:

Bless, Lord, this ring that he/she who gives it and she/he who wears it may abide in your peace. Amen.

Placing the ring upon the woman's finger, the man says:

_____, I love you, and I give you this ring as a sign of my love and faithfulness.

Placing the ring upon the man's finger, the woman says:

_____, I love you, and I give you this ring
as a sign of my love and faithfulness.

Selection S

The minister says:

These rings (symbols)
are the outward and visible sign
of an inward and spiritual grace,
signifying to us the union
between Jesus Christ and his church.

The minister prays:

Bless, O Lord, the giving of these rings (symbols),
that they who wear them may live in your peace,
and continue in your favor all the days of their life,
through Jesus Christ our Lord. Amen.

The giver(s) may say to the recipient(s):

_____,
I give you this ring (symbol)
as a sign of my vow,
and with all that I am,
and all that I have,
I honor you
in the name of the Father,
and of the Son,
and of the Holy Spirit.

Selection T

The minister receives the ring(s) and may say:

Let us pray:

God of steadfast love,
by your blessing,
let these rings (this ring) be to _____ and
_____
a symbol of the vows
which they have made this day;
through Jesus Christ our Lord.
Amen.

As the giver places the ring on the ring finger of the other's left hand, the following words may be said:

_____, I give you this ring
as a sign of our marriage
and of the vows which we have made today.

If only one ring is given, the following may be said by the receiver:

_____, I receive this ring
as a sign of our marriage
and of the vows which we have made today.

Selection U

Pastor:

_____ and _____,
what will you share to symbolize your love?

The groom and bride may name the symbol(s) and present them/it to the pastor, who may hold or place a hand on the symbol(s) and offer one of these or another prayer.

Let us pray.
By (these symbols/this symbol) of covenant promise, Gracious God, remind _____ and
_____ of your encircling love and unending faithfulness that in all their life together they may know joy and peace in one another. Amen.

Groom:

_____,
I give you (this/these) _____
as a sign of my love and faithfulness.

Bride:

I receive (this/these) _____
as a sign of our love and faithfulness.

Bride:

_____,
I give you (this/these) _____
as a sign of my love and faithfulness.

Groom:

I receive (this/these) _____
as a sign of our love and faithfulness.

Category 8:
Declaration of Marriage

Selection A

The minister shall declare:

Forasmuch as you, _____ and _____, have covenanted together according to God's holy ordinance of marriage, and have confirmed the same by making solemn vows before God and this company and by joining hands (and by giving and receiving a ring), I pronounce you husband and wife; in the name of the Father and the Son and the Holy Spirit.

Hereafter the minister, addressing the congregation, shall say:

What therefore God has joined together, let no one put asunder. Amen.

Selection B

Then shall the minister say to all who are present:

By the authority committed unto me as a minister of the church of Christ, I declare that _____ and _____ are now husband and wife, according to the ordinance of God, and the law of the State; in the name of the Father, and of the Son, and of the Holy Spirit. Amen.

Then, causing the husband and wife to join their right hands, the minister shall say:

Whom therefore God hath joined together, let no one put asunder.

Selection C

The minister addresses the congregation:

Before God
and in the presence of this congregation,
_____ and _____ have made
  their solemn vows to each other.
They have confirmed their promises by joining of
  hands
[and by the giving and receiving of rings].
Therefore, I proclaim that they are now husband and
  wife.

Blessed be the Father and the Son and the Holy
  Spirit now and forever.

The minister joins the couple's right hands.

The congregation may join the minister saying:

Those whom God has joined together
let no one separate.

The minister addresses the couple:

As God's own,
clothe yourselves with compassion,
kindness, and patience,
forgiving each other
as the Lord has forgiven you,
and crown all these things with love,
which binds everything together in perfect harmony.
(Colossians 3:12–14)

Selection D

The minister addresses the congregation:

Before God
and in the presence of this congregation,
_____ and _____ have made
   their solemn vows to each other.
They have confirmed their promises by joining of
   hands
[and by the giving and receiving of rings].
Therefore, I proclaim that they are now husband and
   wife.

Blessed be the Father and the Son and the Holy
   Spirit now and forever.

The minister joins the couple's right hands.

The congregation may join the minister saying:

Those whom God has joined together
let no one separate.

Selection E

*The couple shall join their right hands. Then shall the
minister lay his right hand upon their hands and say:*

Forasmuch as _____ and _____
have consented together in holy wedlock, and have
declared the same before God and in the presence of
this company, I pronounce them husband and wife.
In the Name of the Father, and of the Son, and of the
Holy Ghost. Amen.

What God hath joined together, let no one put
   asunder.

*Then may they kneel and the minister may bless them,
saying:*

The Lord God, who created our first parents and
sanctified their union in marriage: Sanctify and bless
you, that you may please him both in body and
soul, and live together in holy love until life's end.
Amen.

Selection F

*Then, the man and woman having joined hands, the
minister shall say:*

_____ and _____, you are now
husband and wife according to the witness of the
holy universal church, and the law of this state. Become one. Fulfill your promises. Love and serve the
Lord.

What God has united, humanity must not divide.

Selection G

*Then shall the minister join their right hands together
and, with his hand on their united hands, shall say:*

Forasmuch as _____ and _____
have consented together in holy wedlock, and have
witnessed the same before God and this company,
and thereto have pledged their faith each to the
other and have declared the same by joining hands
and by giving and receiving rings; I pronounce that
they are husband and wife together, in the name of
the Father, and of the Son, and of the Holy Spirit.
Those whom God hath joined together let no one
put asunder. Amen.

Selection H

*The bride and groom join hands, and the minister
announces their marriage by saying:*

_____ and _____, by their
promises before God and in the presence of this congregation, have bound themselves to one another as
husband and wife.

Blessed be the Father and the Son and the Holy
Spirit now and forever.

Those whom God joined together let no one put
asunder. Amen.

Selection I

The minister shall join their right hands and say:

In the name of God the Father, the Son, and the Holy Spirit, I now join you together to live within the bonds of holy marriage, as husband and wife. What therefore God has joined together, let no one put asunder.

Selection J

The minister shall join the hands of the couple together and say:

Forasmuch as you, _____ and _____, have consented together in this sacred covenant, and have declared the same before God and this company, I pronounce you husband and wife, in the name of the Father, and of the Son, and of the Holy Spirit. Amen.

Selection K

Then the minister may join the hands of the couple and shall say:

Since you have now pledged yourselves to one another in the covenant of marriage, and have made your declaration before God, and these witnesses, I pronounce you to be husband and wife. In the name of the Father, and of the Son, and of the Holy Spirit. Amen.

Selection L

The minister joins the right hands of husband and wife and says:

Now that _____ and _____ have given themselves to each other by solemn vows, with the joining of hands and the giving and receiving of rings, I pronounce that they are husband and wife, in the name of the Father, and of the Son, and of the Holy Spirit.

Those whom God has joined together let no one put asunder.

Selection M

Because _____ and _____ have made their vows with each other before God and all of us here, I declare them to be husband and wife in the name of God, Father, Son, and Holy Spirit. Amen.

Let no one divide those whom God has united.

Selection N

The wife and husband join hands. The minister may place a hand on, or wrap a stole around, their joined hands.

Minister to husband and wife:

You have declared your consent and vows before God and this congregation. May God confirm your covenant and fill you both with grace.

Minister to people:

Now that _____ and _____
have given themselves to each other by solemn vows,
with the joining of hands,
and the giving and receiving of rings,
I announce to you that they are husband and wife
in the name of the Father, and of the Son,
and of the Holy Spirit.

Those whom God has joined together,
let no one put asunder.

Amen.

Selection O

Minister, addressing the couple:

_____ and _____, you have committed yourselves to each other in this joyous covenant. Become one. Fulfill your promises. Love and serve God, honor Christ and each other, and rejoice in the power of the Holy Spirit.

Minister, addressing the congregation:

By their promises made before us this day, _____ and _____ have united themselves as husband and wife in sacred covenant. Those whom God has joined together let no one separate.

Selection P

Minister, addressing the congregation:

Those whom God has joined together let no one separate.

Minister, addressing the couple:

_____ and _____, you are wife and husband with the blessing of Christ's church. Be merciful in all your ways, kind in heart, and humble in mind. Accept life, and be most patient and tolerant with one another. Forgive as freely as God has forgiven you. And, above everything else, be truly loving. Let the peace of Christ rule in your hearts, remembering that as members of one body you are called to live in harmony, and never forget to be thankful for what God has done for you.

Selection Q

The couple join hands.

The minister asks the people to stand, and addresses them:

Hear the words of our Lord Jesus Christ:
From the beginning of creation,
God made them male and female.
For this reason a man shall leave his father and
    mother
and be joined to his wife,
and the two shall become one.
So they are no longer two but one.
Let no one separate those whom God has joined
    together. (Mark 10:6–9)

Before God and in the presence of us all,
_____ and _____ have made
    their solemn vows.
They have confirmed their marriage
by the joining of hands
and by the giving and receiving of rings (a ring).
In the name of the Father,
and of the Son, and of the Holy Spirit,
I therefore proclaim
that they are now husband and wife.

Category 9:
Prayer for the Marriage

Selection A

Couple may kneel.

The minister says:

In peace, let us pray to the Lord.

All grace comes from you, O God,
and you alone are the source of eternal life.
Bless your servants
_____ and _____,
that they may faithfully live together
to the end of their lives.

May they be patient and gentle,
ready to trust each other,
and to face together the challenge of the future.

May they pray together in joy and in sorrow,
and always give thanks for the gift of each other.

Be with them in all their happiness;
that your joy may be in them,
and their joy may be full.

Strengthen them in every time of trouble,
that they may bear each other's burdens,
and so fulfill the law of Christ.

Give _____ and _____ grace,
    when they hurt each other,
to recognize and acknowledge their fault,
to ask for each other's forgiveness,
and to know your mercy and love.

May your peace dwell in their home,
and be a sign of hope for peace in the world.

Let their home be a place of welcome,
that its happiness may be freely shared.

Through loving one another in Christ,
may they be strengthened to love Christ in their
    neighbor.

May they be creative in their daily work,
and find fulfillment in the life of their community.

The following petition may be included:

May _____ and _____ enjoy the
    gift and heritage of children.
Grant that they may be loving and wise parents,
with grace to bring up their children
to know you, to love you, and to serve you.

*The following petition may be included if there are
children/grandchildren of a previous marriage:*

May _____ and _____ enjoy the
    gift and heritage of their children.
Grant them the grace to share their love (and faith)
with _____ and _____ *(names of
    children)*
that they may grow together as a loving family.

Bless the parents and families of _____
    and _____,
that they may be united in love and friendship.

70

Grant that all married people
who have witnessed these vows
today may find their lives strengthened
and their loyalties confirmed.

We ask these prayers in the name of Christ our Lord.
Amen.

Selection B

Couple may kneel.

The minister says:

Let us pray.

Most merciful and gracious God, of whom the whole family in heaven and earth is named: Give to these your servants the seal of your approval, and your fatherly love; granting to them grace to fulfill, with pure and steadfast affection, the vow and covenant made between them. Guide them together, we pray, in the way of righteousness and peace, that, loving and serving you, with one heart and mind, all the days of their life, they may be abundantly enriched with the token of your everlasting favor, in Jesus Christ our Lord. Amen.

Selection C

Couple may kneel.

The minister says:

Let us pray.

Eternal God,
creator and preserver of all life,
author of salvation
and giver of all grace:

look with favor upon the world you have made and
    redeemed,
and especially upon _____ and

_____ .

Give them wisdom and devotion in their common
    life,
that each may be to the other

a strength in need,
a comfort in sorrow,
a counselor in perplexity,
and a companion in joy.

Grant that their wills may be so knit together in your
    will,
and their spirits in your Spirit,
that they may grow in love and peace
with you and each other
all the days of their life.

Give them courage,
when they hurt each other,
to recognize and confess their fault,
and the grace to seek your forgiveness,
and to forgive each other.

Make their life together
a sign of Christ's love to this sinful and broken world,
that unity may overcome estrangement,
forgiveness heal guilt,
and joy conquer despair.

Give them such fulfillment of their mutual love
that they may reach out in concern for others.

[Give to them, if it is your will,
the gift of children,
and the wisdom to bring them up
to know you, to love you,
and to serve you.]

Grant that all who have witnessed these vows today
may find their lives strengthened,
and that all who are married
may depart with their own promises renewed.

Enrich with your grace
all husbands and wives, parents and children,
that, loving and supporting one another,
they may serve those in need
and be a sign of your kingdom.

Grant that the bonds of our common humanity,
by which all your children are united one to another,
may be so transformed by your Spirit
that your peace and justice may fill the earth,
through Jesus Christ our Lord. Amen.

Selection D

Couple may kneel.

The minister says:

Let us pray.

Eternal God,
without your grace no promise is sure.
Strengthen _____ and _____
    with patience, kindness,
gentleness, and all other gifts of your Spirit,
so that they may fulfill the vows they have made.
Keep them faithful to each other and to you.
Fill them with such love and joy
that they may build a home of peace and welcome.
Guide them by your word
to serve you all their days.

Enable us all, O God,
in each of our homes and lives to do your will.
Enrich us with your grace so that,
encouraging and supporting one another,
we may serve those in need
and hasten the coming of peace, love, and justice on
    earth,
through Jesus Christ our Lord.

Amen.

Selection E

Couple may kneel.

The minister says:

Let us pray.

Almighty and most merciful God, who has now united _____ and _____ in holy marriage: grant them your grace to live according to your holy word; strengthen them in constant faithfulness and true affection toward each other; sustain and defend them in the midst of their trials and temptations; and help them to live this life in faith toward you, in the context of your church, and in loving service for one another, that they may enjoy the fruits of the Christian life; through Jesus Christ our Lord. Amen.

Selection F

Couple may kneel.

The minister says:

Let us pray.

Eternal God: without your grace no promise is sure. Strengthen _____ and _____ with the gift of your Spirit, so they may fulfill the vows they have taken. Keep them faithful to each other and to you. Fill them with such love and joy that they may build a home where no one is a stranger. And guide them by your word to serve you all the days of their lives; through Jesus Christ our Lord, to whom be honor and glory forever and ever. Amen.

Selection G

Couple may kneel.

The minister says:

Let us pray.

O eternal God, creator and preserver of all humanity, giver of all spiritual grace, the author of everlasting life: Send your blessings upon _____ and _____, whom we bless in your name; that they may surely perform and keep the vow and covenant between them made, and may ever remain in perfect love and peace together, and live according to your laws.

Look graciously upon them, that they may love, honor, and cherish each other, and so live together in faithfulness and patience, in wisdom and true godliness, that their home may be a haven of blessing and a place of peace; through Jesus Christ our Lord. Amen.

Selection H

Couple may kneel.

The minister says:

Let us bless God for all the gifts in which we rejoice today.

Lord God, constant in mercy, great in faithfulness: With high praise we recall your acts of unfailing love for the human family, for the house of Israel, and for your people the church.

We bless you for the joy which your servants, _____ and _____, have found in each other, and pray that you give to us such a sense of your constant love that we may employ all our strength in a life of praise of you, whose work alone holds true and endures forever. Amen.

Let us pray for _____ and _____ in their life together.

Faithful Lord, source of love, pour down your grace upon _____ and _____, that they may fulfill the vows they have made this day and reflect your steadfast love in their lifelong faithfulness to each other. As members with them of the body of Christ, use us to support their life together; and from your great store of strength give them power and patience, affection and understanding, courage, and love toward you, toward each other, and toward the world, that they may continue together in mutual growth according to your will in Jesus Christ our Lord. Amen.

Other intercessions may be offered:

Let us pray for all families throughout the world.

Gracious Father, you bless the family and renew your people. Enrich husbands and wives, parents and children more and more with your grace, that, strengthening and supporting each other, they may serve those in need and be a sign of the fulfillment of your perfect kingdom, where with your Son Jesus Christ, and the Holy Spirit, you live and reign, one God through all ages of ages. Amen.

Selection I

Couple may kneel.

The minister says:

Let us pray.

Most merciful and gracious God, we thank you for the love which binds men and women together, and especially for the institution of marriage, the tenderness of its ties and the sacredness of its obligations. Look with favor upon these your servants; sanctify and bless their union; grant them grace to fulfill, with pure and steadfast affection, the vow and covenant made between them. Guide them together in the way of righteousness and peace, that loving and serving you, with one heart and mind, they may be abundantly enriched by your grace; through Jesus Christ our Lord. Amen.

Selection J

Couple may kneel.

The minister says:

Let us pray.

Eternal God, whose love is the source of all good things; we pray that knowledge of your love will inspire the union which has now begun. Grant that _____ and _____, who have been joined in your name, may live in harmony and true companionship throughout their life together — seeking one another's welfare, bearing one another's burdens, and sharing one another's joys. Give them the resources to live without fear of poverty, and grant them joy in their home. Father, keep them true to the faith in which this marriage has begun, that they may always walk within the light and love of Christ, strengthened by the Spirit against all temptation; and when mortal life is over, bring them in your mercy to the joy of that life which shall have no ending, in the kingdom of our Lord and Savior, Jesus Christ. Amen.

Selection K

Couple may kneel.

The minister says:

Let us pray.

Almighty and everlasting Father, who has given to humankind the ordinance of marriage, and made it holy with your blessing: Bless, your servants, _____ and _____, now joined together as husband and wife; and grant that, bearing one another's burdens, sharing one another's joys, and together fulfilling the duties of their home, they may ever be faithful to each other in love and obedience to your word; through Jesus Christ our Lord. Amen.

Selection L

Couple may kneel.

The minister says:

Let us pray.

O Lord and Savior Jesus Christ, who did share at Nazareth the life of an earthly home: Be present in the home of these your servants as Lord and King; give them grace that they may minister to others as you minister to men and women, and grant that by deed and word they may be witnesses of your saving love to those with whom they live; for your holy name's sake, who lives and reigns with the Father and the Holy Spirit, one God, world without end. Amen.

Selection M

Couple may kneel.

The minister says:

Let us pray.

Eternal God, creator and preserver of all life, author of salvation, and giver of all grace: Look with favor upon the world you have made, and for which

your Son gave his life, and especially upon this man and this woman whom you make one flesh in holy matrimony. Amen.

Give them wisdom and devotion in the ordering of their common life, that each may be to the other a strength in need, a counselor in perplexity, a comfort in sorrow, and a companion in joy. Amen.

Grant that their wills may be so knit together in your will, and their spirits in your Spirit, that they may grow in love and peace with you and one another all the days of their life. Amen.

Give them grace, when they hurt each other, to recognize and acknowledge their fault, and to seek each other's forgiveness and yours. Amen.

Make their life together a sign of Christ's love to this sinful and broken world, that unity may overcome estrangement, forgiveness heal guilt, and joy conquer despair. Amen.

[Bestow on them, if it is your will, the gift and heritage of children, and the grace to bring them up to know you, to love you, and to serve you. Amen.]

Give them such fulfillment of their mutual affection that they may reach out in love and concern for others. Amen.

Grant that all married persons who have witnessed these vows may find their lives strengthened and their loyalties confirmed. Amen.

Grant that the bonds of our common humanity, by which all your children are united one to another, and the living to the dead, may be so transformed by your grace, that your will may be done on earth as it is in heaven; where, O Father, with your Son and the Holy Spirit, you live and reign in perfect unity, now and for ever. Amen.

Selection N

Couple may kneel.

The minister says:

Let us pray.

O God, you have so consecrated the covenant of marriage that in it is represented the spiritual unity between Christ and his church: Send therefore your blessing upon these your servants, that they may so love, honor, and cherish each other in faithfulness and patience, in wisdom and true godliness, that their home may be a haven of blessing and peace; through Jesus Christ our Lord, who lives and reigns with you and the Holy Spirit, one God, now and for ever. Amen.

Selection O

Couple may kneel.

The minister says:

Let us pray.

O God, you have so consecrated the covenant of Christian marriage that in it is represented the covenant between Christ and his church. Send therefore your blessing upon _____ and _____, that they may surely keep their marriage covenant and so grow in love and godliness together, that their home may be a haven of blessing and peace, through Jesus Christ our Lord. Amen.

Selection P

Couple may kneel.

The minister says:

Let us ask for the blessing of the Lord.

Eternal God,
in whom we live and move and have our being;
bless _____ and _____
that they may live together in marriage
according to the vows they have made before you.

Bless them with your love,
that their love for each other
may grow ever deeper,
and their love for you may shine forth
before the world.

Bless them with your mercy,
that they may be patient and caring,

willing to share each other's joys and sorrows,
to forgive and to be forgiven,
in their life together and in the world.

Bless them with your peace,
that they may be calm and sure,
trusting in you with confident heart
and living in harmony and concord
and within their family and among all people.

Bless them with your presence,
that within their hearts and their home
Christ may reign as head,
and that they may acknowledge his lordship
with praise and thanksgiving now,
and through all their life together,
to the glory of your holy name! Amen.

Selection Q

Couple may kneel.

The minister says:

Let us pray.

O God, creator of life, author of salvation and giver of all good gifts; look with favor upon _____ and _____ who have covenanted marriage in your name. Bless their union, and sustain them in their devotion to each other and to you.

Grant them the desire to order their lives according to your will, that in their relationship with each other, and those around them, they may show forth the joy and peace of Christ.

Sustain them in the seasons and conditions of their lives by the power of your Holy Spirit, that in joy and sorrow, leisure and labor, plenty and want, they may give thanks for your steadfast love and declare your faithfulness before the world.

Increase in them the will to grow in faith and service to Christ. Let their life together bear witness to the healing and reconciling love of Christ for this troubled, broken world.

Give them a deep appreciation of the unity of all persons within your creation, that their love for each other may be reflected also in their desire for justice, dignity, and meaning for all your children.

Keep ever vivid in their hearts a vision of your kingdom, and enable them to live in the hope of its fulfillment. By the power of your Spirit, O God, accomplish these petitions as they accord with your will, for we pray through Jesus Christ our Lord. Amen.

Selection R

Couple may kneel.

The minister says:

Let us pray.

Most gracious God, we give you thanks for your tender love. You sent Jesus Christ to come among us, to be born of a human mother, and to make the way of the cross into the way of life. We thank you, too, for consecrating the union of a man and a woman in Christ's name.

By the power of your Holy Spirit, pour out the abundance of your blessing on _____ and _____. Defend them from every enemy. Lead them into all peace. Let their love for each other be a seal on their hearts, a mantle about their shoulders, and a crown on their heads. Bless them in their work and in their companionship, in their sleeping and in their waking, in their joys and in their sorrows, in their lives and in their deaths. Nurture them in a community of the faithful gathered about you. Through Jesus Christ our Lord. Amen.

Selection S

Couple may kneel.

The minister says:

Let us pray.

Merciful God, we thank you for your love that lives within us and calls us from loneliness to compan-

ionship. We thank you for all who have gone before us: for Adam and Eve, for Sarah and Abraham, for Joseph and Mary, and for countless parents whose names we do not know.

We thank you for our own parents, and for all, whether married or single, who are mother or father to us, as we grow to the fullness of the stature of Christ.

Bless _____ and _____, that they may have the grace to live the promises they have made. Defend them from all enemies of their love. Teach them the patience of undeserved forgiveness. Bring them to old age, rejoicing in love's winter more fully than in its springtime.

•

The following words of the prayer may be used if children are present who will share in the couple's household. If these words are not used, continue with the closing of the prayer.

Bless (this child/these children), _____ _____, that (he/she/they) may find in this new home a haven of love and joy where Jesus Christ is honored in kind words and tender deeds.

•

Finally, in your mercy, bring _____ and _____ to that table where your saints feast for ever in your heavenly home; through Jesus Christ our sovereign Savior who, with you and the Holy Spirit, lives and reigns, one God, forever and ever. Amen.

Selection T

Couple may kneel.

The minister says:

Let us pray.

O faithful God, who keeps your covenant and truth with those that love you, hear the marriage vow which these servants, _____ and _____, have made with you. Grant to them the grace of your good Spirit, that with all faithfulness they may observe and keep these vows; walking together in faith, being led by the Spirit of your presence and strengthened by your hand, all the days of their lives; through Jesus Christ our Lord. Amen.

Selection U

Couple may kneel.

The minister says:

Let us pray for _____ and _____
in their life together:

Most gracious God,
we bless you for your tender love
in sending Jesus Christ to come among us,
born of a human mother.
We give you thanks that he grew up
in a home in Nazareth,
and joined in the celebration of a marriage
in Cana of Galilee.
By the power of the Holy Spirit,
give your blessing to
_____ and _____.
Let their love for each other
be a seal upon their hearts,
a mantle about their shoulders,
and a crown upon their heads.
Bless them in their work and in their companionship,
in their joys and in their sorrows.
And finally in your mercy
bring them to your heavenly home;
through Jesus Christ our Lord. Amen.

Selection V

Couple may kneel.

The minister says:

Let us pray.

Faithful Lord, source of all love,
pour down your grace upon _____ and
_____,

that they may fulfill the vows they have made today,
and reflect your steadfast love
in their lifelong faithfulness to each other.
Help us to support them in their life together.
Give them courage and patience,
affection and understanding,
and love toward you,
toward each other,
and toward the world;
that they may continue to grow
in Jesus Christ our Lord.
Amen.

Selection W

Couple may kneel.

The minister says:

Let us pray.

Creator God, giver of life,
bless _____ and _____ whom
    you have joined in marriage.
Grant them wisdom and devotion in their life together,
that each may be for the other a strength in need,
a comfort in sorrow, and a companion in joy.
So unite their wills in your will,
and their spirits in your Spirit,
that they may live and grow together in love and
    peace
all the days of their life.

Gracious God,
you have called us to live in loving families,
and by your generous love
all the families on earth are blessed.
We pray today for the parents and families of
_____ and _____.
We recall the gracious influences and loving deeds
that have surrounded
_____ and _____
in their homes.
And for their parents we ask continuing health,
fulfillment of life,
and the joy of knowing their children's children.

Gracious Father,
you bless family life and renew your people.
Enrich husbands and wives, parents and children,
more and more with your grace,
that, strengthening and supporting each other,
they may serve those in need
and be a sign of the fulfillment of your kingdom,
where, with your Son Jesus Christ and the Holy
    Spirit,
you live and reign, one God through all ages.
Amen.

Selection X

Couple may kneel.

The minister says:

Let us pray.

Most gracious God, we give you thanks for your tender love in sending Jesus Christ to come among us, to be born of a human mother, and to make the way of the cross to be the way of life. We thank you, also, for consecrating the union of man and woman in his Name. By the power of your Holy Spirit, pour out the abundance of your blessing upon this man and this woman. Defend them from every enemy. Lead them into all peace. Let their love for each other be a seal upon their hearts, a mantle about their shoulders, and a crown upon their foreheads. Bless them in their work and in their companionship; in their sleeping and in their waking; in their joys and in their sorrows; in their life and in their death. Finally, in your mercy, bring them to that table where your saints feast for ever in your heavenly home: through Jesus Christ our Lord, who with you and the Holy Spirit lives and reigns, one God, for ever and ever. Amen.

Selection Y

Couple may kneel.

The minister says:

Let us pray.

O God, Creator and Father of us all, we thank you for the gift of life — and, in life, for the gift of marriage. We praise and thank you for all the joys that can come to men and women through marriage, and for the blessings of home and family.

Today, especially, we think of _____ and _____ as they begin their life together as husband and wife. With them we thank you for the joy they find in each other. Give them strength, Father, to keep the vows they have made and cherish the love they share, that they may be faithful and devoted. Help them support each other with patience, understanding, and honesty. (Teach them to be wise and loving parents of any children they may have.) (We pray for their parents, that at this moment of parting they may rejoice in their children's happiness.)

Look with favor, God, on all our homes. Defend them from every evil that may threaten them, from outside or within. Let your Spirit so direct all of us that we may each look to the good of others in word and deed and grow in grace as we advance in years, through Jesus Christ our Lord. Amen.

Category 10:
The Lord's Prayer

Selection A

The minister says:

Let us pray the prayer our Lord taught us saying:

Our Father, who art in heaven, hallowed be thy name. Thy kingdom come. Thy will be done on earth as it is in heaven. Give us this day our daily bread. And forgive us our debts, as we forgive our debtors. And lead us not into temptation, but deliver us from evil; for thine is the kingdom, and the power, and the glory, forever. Amen.

Selection B

The minister says:

Let us pray the prayer our Lord taught us saying:

Our Father, who art in heaven, hallowed be thy name. Thy kingdom come, thy will be done on earth as it is in heaven. Give us this day our daily bread. And forgive us our trespasses, as we forgive those who trespass against us. And lead us not into temptation, but deliver us from evil. For thine is the kingdom, and the power, and the glory, forever. Amen.

Selection C

The minister says:

Let us pray the prayer our Lord taught us saying:

Our Father, who art in heaven, hallowed be thy name, thy kingdom come, thy will be done, on earth as it is in heaven. Give us this day our daily bread; and forgive us our trespasses, as we forgive those who trespass against us; and lead us not into temptation, but deliver us from evil. For thine is the kingdom, and the power, and the glory, forever and ever. Amen.

Selection D

The minister says:

Let us pray the prayer our Lord taught us saying:

Our Father in heaven,
   hallowed be your name,
   your kingdom come,
   your will be done,
     on earth as in heaven.
Give us today our daily bread.
Forgive us our sins
   as we forgive those
     who sin against us.
Save us from the time of trial
   and deliver us from evil.
For the kingdom, the power,
   and the glory are yours,
     now and forever. Amen.

Category 11:
Benediction

Selection A

The minister says:

The peace of God that passes all understanding keep your hearts and minds in the knowledge and love of God and of his Son Jesus Christ; and the blessing of God almighty, the Father and the Son and the Holy Spirit, be upon you and remain with you always. Amen.

Selection B

The minister says:

The Lord bless you and keep you.
The Lord make his face to shine upon you, and give you peace.
The Lord lift up his countenance upon you, and give you peace.
The grace of our Lord Jesus Christ be with you. Amen.

Selection C

The minister says:

The grace of the Lord Jesus Christ and the love of God and the fellowship of the Holy Spirit be with you. Amen.

Selection D

The minister says:

The grace of the Lord Jesus Christ and the love of God and the fellowship of the Holy Spirit be with you, both now and forever. Amen.

Selection E

The minister says:

The Lord bless you and keep you; the Lord make his face to shine upon you, and be gracious unto you; the Lord lift up his countenance upon you, and give you peace: both now and in the life everlasting. Amen.

Selection F

The minister says:

God the Father, God the Son, God the Holy Spirit, bless, preserve, and keep you, the Lord mercifully with his favor look upon you, and fill you with all spiritual benediction and grace; that you may so live together in this life that in the world to come you may have life everlasting. Amen.

Selection G

This benediction should not be used if you choose Selection C in Category 8.

The minister says:

As God's own,
clothe yourselves with compassion,
kindness, and patience,
forgiving each other
as the Lord has forgiven you,
and crown all these things with love,
which binds everything together in perfect harmony.
Amen.

Selection H

The minister says:

Whatever you do, in word or deed,
do everything in the name of the Lord Jesus,
giving thanks to God through him.
Amen.

Selection I

The minister says:

The grace of Christ attend you,
the love of God surround you,
the Holy Spirit keep you,
that you may live in faith,
abound in hope,
and grow in love,
both now and forevermore.
Amen.

Selection J

The minister says:

The Lord bless you and keep you.
The Lord make his face shine upon you, and be
    gracious unto you.
The Lord lift up his countenance upon you,
and give you peace. Amen.

Selection K

The minister says:

Glory be to him who can keep you from falling and bring you safe to his glorious presence, innocent and happy. To God, the only God, who saves us through Jesus Christ our Lord, be the glory, majesty, authority, and power, which he had before time began, now and forever. Amen.

Selection L

The minister says:

God, the Father, the Son, and the Holy Spirit, bless, preserve, and keep you; the Lord graciously with his favor look upon you, and so fill you with all spiritual benediction and love that you may so live together in this life that in the world to come you may have life everlasting. Amen.

Selection M

The minister says:

Almighty God, Father, Son, and Holy Spirit, keep you in his light and truth and love now and forever. Amen.

Selection N

The minister says:

God Almighty send you his light and truth to keep you all the days of your life. The hand of God protect you; his holy Angels accompany you. God the Father, God the Son, and God the Holy Ghost, cause his grace to be mighty upon you. Amen.

Selection O

The minister says:

The Lord bless you and keep you;
The Lord make his face shine upon you, and be
    gracious unto you;

The Lord lift up his countenance upon you, and give
you peace:
In the name of Jesus. Amen.

Selection P

The minister says:

The peace of God, which passes all understanding,
keep your hearts and minds in the knowledge and
love of God, and of his Son Jesus Christ our Lord;
and the blessing of God Almighty, the Father, the
Son, and the Holy Spirit, be with you, and remain
with you always. Amen.

Selection Q

The minister says:

God the Father, God the Son, God the Holy Spirit,
bless, preserve, and keep you; the Lord mercifully
with his favor look upon you, and fill you with all
spiritual benediction and grace; that you may faithfully live together in this life, and in the age to come
have life everlasting. Amen.

Selection R

The minister says:

Go in peace and may we love the Lord our God
with all our heart, mind, soul, and strength; and our
neighbor as ourselves. In the name of the Father, and
of the Son, and of the Holy Spirit. Amen.

Selection S

The minister says:

Almighty God, Father, Son, and Holy Spirit, direct
and keep you in his light and truth and love all the
days of your life. Amen.

Selection T

The minister says:

God the eternal keep you in love with each other, so
that the peace of Christ may abide in your home. Go
to serve God and your neighbor in all that you do.

Bear witness to the love of God in this world so that
those to whom love is a stranger will find in you generous friends. The grace of the Lord Jesus Christ, the
love of God, and the communion of the Holy Spirit
be with you all. Amen.

Selection U

The minister says:

Go forth in the love of God; go forth in hope and joy,
knowing that God is with you always.

And the peace of God, which passes all understanding, keep your hearts and minds in the knowledge
and love of God and of Christ Jesus; and the blessing
of god, Creator, Redeemer, and Sanctifier, be with
you, and remain with you always. Amen.

Notes to Part 1

ENDNOTE KEY

AUS   The Uniting Church in Australia, "The Marriage Service," in *Uniting in Worship* (Melbourne: Uniting Church Press, 1988).

CAN   The United Church of Canada, "An Order for the Solemnization of Matrimony," in *The Book of Common Order of the United Church of Canada* (Toronto: United Church Publishing House, 1950).

E   Protestant Episcopal Church in the United States of America, "The Form of Solemnization of Matrimony," in *The Book of Common Prayer* (New York: Church Hymnal Corp., 1945).

EC2   The Evangelical Covenant Church of America, "Rite of Marriage II," in *The Covenant Book of Worship* (Chicago: Covenant Press, 1981).

ED   Rev. Emily Duncan Rosencrans and the Rev. Andrew Rosencrans, Wedding service written for their own wedding. Biblical quotation from the Book of Ruth.

E79   The Episcopal Church, "The Celebration and Blessing of a Marriage," in *The Book of Common Prayer* (New York: Seabury Press, 1979).

I   International Commission on English in the Liturgy (ICEL), *Rite of Marriage* (1969).

L   The United Lutheran Church of America, "Lutheran Marriage Service" (Minneapolis: Augsburg Publishing House, n.d.). Copyright © United Lutheran Church in America. Used by permission of Augsburg Fortress.

L58   The Lutheran Churches cooperating in the Commission on the Liturgy and Hymnal, "Order for Marriage," in *Service Book and Hymnal* (Minneapolis: Augsburg Publishing House, 1958).

L78   Lutheran Church in America et al., "Marriage," in *Lutheran Book of Worship* (Minneapolis: Augsburg Publishing House, 1978).

MOR   Moravian Church, "Solemnization of Matrimony," in *Hymnal and Liturgies of the Moravian Church* (Bethlehem, Pa.: Department of Publications, Moravian Church, Northern Province, 1969).

MTH   The United Methodist Church, "The Order for the Service of Marriage," in *The Book of Worship of the United Methodist Church* (Nashville: Abingdon Press, 1964, 1965).

M85   The United Methodist Church, "A Service of Christian Marriage," in *The Book of Services* (Nashville: United Methodist Publishing House, 1985).

OF   Rev. and Mrs. Deryl Fleming and Dr. Wayne E. Oates, "A Baptist Service," in Perry Biddle, *Abingdon Marriage Manual* (Nashville: Abingdon Press, 1974). Used by permission.

P   Presbyterian Church in the United States of America, "Order for the Solemnization of Marriage," in *The Book of Common Worship* (Philadelphia: Westminster Press, 1946).

P72   The Joint Committee on Worship for Cumberland Presbyterian Church, Presbyterian Church in the United States, and the United Presbyterian Church in the United States of America, "The Marriage Service," in *The Worshipbook: Services and Hymns* (Philadelphia: Westminster Press, 1970, 1972).

P86   Presbyterian Church (U.S.A.) and the Cumberland Presbyterian Church, "Christian Marriage: Rite I — A Service for General Use," in *Christian Marriage: The Worship of God,* Supplemental Liturgical Resource 3 (Philadelphia: Westminster Press, 1986).

RCA   Reformed Church in America, "Order of Service for the Solemnization of Marriage," in *The Liturgy of the Reformed Church in America, Together with the Psalter,* ed. Gerrit T. Vander Lugt (Grandville, Mich.: Reformed Church Press, 1968).

RCA87   Reformed Church in America, "Order of Worship for Christian Marriage," in *Worship the Lord* (Grandville, Mich.: Reformed Church Press, 1987).

SCT   Church of Scotland, "First Order for the Celebration of Marriage," in *The Book of Common Order (1979)* (Edinburgh: Saint Andrew Press, 1979).

SI   Church of South India, "The Marriage Service," in *The Book of Common Worship* (London: Oxford University Press, 1963).

SU   Source Unknown.

UCC   United Church of Christ, "The Order for Marriage," in *Services of the Church* (New York: United Church Press, 1969).

UCC86   United Church of Christ, "Order for Marriage," in *Book of Worship* (New York: United Church of Christ Office for Church Life and Leadership, 1986).

SELECTION RESOURCES

Category 1

A. RCA87 variation
B. OF variation
C. P86
D. AUS variation
E. MTH variation
F. UCC86 variation
G. UCC86 variation
H. E79 variation
I. P variation
J. L58 variation
K. RCA variation
L. RCA
M. MTH variation
N. E79
O. P variation
P. SI
Q. SI variation
R. UCC
S. MTH
T. MOR
U. MOR variation
V. CAN
W. CAN variation
X. SCT
Y. SCT variation
Z. E79
AA. E variation
BB. UCC variation
CC. EC2
DD. M85

Category 2

A. EC2
B. 1 Corinthians 13:4–7 (RSV)
C. P86
D. P72
E. P72
F. MTH
G. MTH variation
H. L78
I. UCC
J. UCC variation
K. SCT
L. SCT variation
M. SI
N. SI variation

Category 3

A. RCA variation
B. P86
C. UCC
D. P variation
E. SCT variation
F. SI variation
G. E79
H. SU
I. EC2 variation
J. UCC86
K. EC2
L. EC2 variation
M. M85
N. AUS

O. I

P. UCC86

Category 4

A. P variation

B. P variation

C. P86 variation

D. P86 variation

E. L variation

F. L variation

G. MTH variation

H. MOR

I. MOR variation

J. UCC

K. SI

L. SI variation

M. UCC86

N. E79 variation

O. EC2

P. M85

Q. RCA87

R. AUS

Category 5

A. RCA87

B. RCA87 variation

C. UCC86

D. RCA variation

E. RCA variation

F. RCA variation

G. P86

H. P86 variation

I. P86 variation

J. P86 variation

K. P86

L. P86 variation

M. P86 variation

N. P86 variation

O. L

P. L58

Q. L58 variation

R. SI

S. E79 variation

T. E79 variation

U. EC2

V. EC2 variation

W. M85

X. M85 variation

Y. M85 variation

Z. RCA

AA. RCA variation

BB. RCA variation

CC. AUS

DD. AUS

EE. AUS

Category 6

A. RCA

B. RCA variation

C. P variation

D. P86

E. P86

F. L variation

G. P72

H. P72

I. MTH

J. MTH variation

K. L78

L. L variation

M. MOR variation

N. UCC

O. SCT

P. SCT

Q. SI variation

R. E79

S. AUS

T. EC2

U. ED

V. EC2

W. M85

X. RCA87

Y. RCA87

Z. UCC86

AA. AUS

BB. AUS

CC. AUS

Category 7

A. RCA

B. RCA

C. P

D. P variation

E. UCC86

F. P86

G. P86

H. L variation

I. L variation

J. P72

K. MTH

L. UCC

M. UCC

N. SCT

O. SI

P. E79

Q. E79

R. EC2

S. M85

T. AUS

U. UCC86

Category 8

A. RCA

B. P

C. P86

D. P86

E. L variation

F. P72

G. MTH variation

H. L58

I. MOR variation

J. UCC

K. SCT

L. E79

M. EC2

N. M85

O. UCC86

P. UCC86

Q. AUS

Category 9

A. AUS

B. P variation

C. P86

D. P86

E. L variation

F. P72

G. MTH

H. L58

I. MOR variation

J. SCT

K. SI variation

L. SI variation

M. E79

N. E79

O. M85

P. RCA87

Q. RCA87

R. UCC86

S. UCC86

T. RCA variation

U. AUS

V. AUS

W. AUS

X. E79

Y. EC2

Category 11

I. P86

K. P72

O. M85

U. UCC86

Part II

*Wedding
Services
from
Protestant
Churches*

Wedding Services from Protestant Churches

Church of Scotland

Church of South India*

Episcopal (1945)

Episcopal (1979)

Evangelical Covenant Church of America

Lutheran (1958)

Lutheran (1978)

Methodist (1964)

Methodist (1985)

Moravian

Presbyterian (1946)

Presbyterian (1970)

Presbyterian (1986)

Reformed Church in America (1968)

Reformed Church in America (1987)

United Church of Canada (1950)

United Church of Canada (1985, Rite I)

United Church of Canada (1985, Rite II)

United Church of Christ (1969)

United Church of Christ (1986)

Uniting Church in Australia

---

* The Church of South India united former Anglicans, Presbyterians, Congregationalists, and Methodists.

Church of Scotland Wedding Service

FIRST ORDER FOR THE CELEBRATION OF MARRIAGE

The service may begin with the singing of a suitable Hymn during which the minister may lead in the bride. The bridegroom standing on the right side of the bride and at least two witnesses being present the minister shall say:

Unless the Lord builds the house, its builders will have toiled in vain.

Our help is in the name of the Lord, Maker of heaven and earth.

Beloved, we have come together in the house of God to celebrate the marriage of this man and this woman, in the assurance that the Lord Jesus Christ, whose power was revealed at the wedding in Cana of Galilee, is present with us here in all his power and his love.

Marriage is provided by God as part of his loving purpose for humanity since the beginning of creation. Jesus said, "The Creator made them from the beginning male and female. For this reason a man shall leave his father and mother, and be made one with his wife: and the two shall become one flesh."

Marriage is enriched by God for all who have faith in the Gospel, for through the saving grace of Christ and the renewal of the Holy Spirit husband and wife can love one another as Christ loves them.

Marriage is thus a gift and calling of God and is not to be undertaken lightly or from selfish motives but with reverence and dedication, with faith in the en- abling power of Christ, and with due awareness of the purpose for which it is appointed by God.

Marriage is appointed that there may be lifelong companionship, comfort and joy between husband and wife.

It is appointed as the right and proper setting for the full expression of physical love between man and woman.

It is appointed for the ordering of family life, where children — who are also God's gifts to us — may enjoy the security of love and the heritage of faith.

It is appointed for the well-being of human society, which can be stable and happy only where the marriage bond is honored and upheld.

Then addressing the couple the minister shall say:

_____ and _____ you seek to be joined in marriage. I am required to ask you, if you know any reason why you may not lawfully be married to each other, to declare it now.

Since no such reason has been declared let us ask God's blessing on this union. Let us pray.

Almighty Father, Lord of heaven and earth, we praise thee for thy goodness and for thy many gifts. Thy power created us, thy Son redeemed us, thy Spirit sets us free to love. For the richness and variety of life; for the providence which guides us and directs our path; and for the happiness of deep relationships with one another, we give thanks to thee. Especially today we bless thee for the gift of marriage, by which human love is hallowed and made perfect. For the joy that _____ and _____ have found in one another, and for the love and trust in which they enter this covenant of marriage, we give thanks to thee, Lord God.

Give them thy Spirit that the vows they make to one another in thy presence may be the beginning of a true and life-long union. We ask this in the name of Jesus Christ, the Lord of life. Amen.

Then, the congregation standing, the minister shall say to the bride and bridegroom:

As a seal to the vows you are about to make, give each other the right hand.

Then they shall say after him:

I, _____, now take you, _____, to be my wife. In the presence of God and before these witnesses I promise to be a loving, faithful and loyal husband to you, until God shall separate us by death.

I, _____, now take you, _____, to be my husband. In the presence of God and before these witnesses I promise to be a loving, faithful and loyal wife to you, until God shall separate us by death.

Alternatively, this form may be used:

Do you, _____, now take _____ to be your wife; and do you promise, in the presence of God and before these witnesses, to be a loving, faithful and loyal husband to her, until God shall separate you by death?

Answer: I do.

Do you, _____, now take _____ to be your husband; and do you promise, in the presence of God and before these witnesses, to be a loving, faithful and loyal wife to him, until God shall separate you by death?

Answer: I do.

Here the ring(s) shall be given to the minister, who shall return it (them) saying:

As a token of the covenant into which you have entered, *this ring is* given and received.

The ring(s) being placed on the fourth finger of the left hand the minister shall say:

By this sign you take each other, to have and to hold from this day forward, for better, for worse; for richer, for poorer; in sickness and in health; to love and to cherish, till death do you part.

Then the minister may join the hands of the couple and shall say:

Since you have now pledged yourselves to one another in the covenant of marriage, and have made your declaration before God and these witnesses, I pronounce you to be husband and wife. In the name of the Father, and of the Son, and of the Holy Spirit. Amen.

Those whom God has joined together, man must not separate.

Then he shall bless them as they kneel, saying:

God the Father, God the Son, God the Holy Spirit, bless, preserve, and keep you. The Lord pour out the riches of his grace upon you, that you may please him, and live together in holy love until your lives' end. Amen.

or

The Lord bless you and keep you, the Lord make his face to shine upon you, and be gracious unto you. The Lord lift up his countenance upon you, and give you peace, both now and evermore. Amen.

Then a Hymn may be sung.

Here Scripture shall be read.

A short address may be given.

Then the minister shall say:

Let us pray.

Eternal God, whose love is the source of all good things; we pray that knowledge of thy love will inspire the union which has now begun. Grant that those who have been joined in thy name may live in harmony and true companionship throughout their life together — seeking one another's welfare, bearing one another's burdens, and sharing one another's joys. (Bless their union with the gift of children.) Give them the resources to live without the fear of poverty, and grant them joy in their (new) home. Father, keep them true to the faith in which this marriage has begun, that they may always walk within the light and love of Christ, strengthened by the Spirit against all temptation; and when mortal life is over, bring them in thy mercy to the joy of that life which shall have no ending, in the kingdom of our Lord and Savior, Jesus Christ.

Our Father . . .

Then a Hymn may be sung after which the minister pronounces the Benediction.

The peace of God, which passes all understanding, keep your hearts and minds in the knowledge and love of God, and of his Son Jesus Christ our Lord; and the blessing of God Almighty, the Father, the Son, and the Holy Spirit, be among you, and remain with you always. Amen.

Source: *The Book of Common Order (1979)*. The Committee on Public Worship and Aids to Devotion of the Church of Scotland. Edinburgh: Saint Andrew Press, 1979.

Church of South India Wedding Service

THE MARRIAGE SERVICE

Introduction

A lyric or hymn is sung.

The persons to be married present themselves before the minister, the man standing at the right hand of the woman.

The minister says:

Dearly beloved, we are gathered here in the presence of God to join this man and this woman in marriage. This is a way of life instituted by God, and Holy Scripture commands all men to hold it in honor. Our Lord Jesus Christ blessed it by his presence at Cana of Galilee.

About this way of life, hear what our Lord says:

> From the beginning of creation, "God made them male and female." "For this reason a man shall leave his father and mother and be joined to his wife, and the two shall become one." So they are no longer two but one. What therefore God has joined together, let not man put asunder. (Mark 10:6–9)

Marriage is therefore not by any to be undertaken lightly or ill-advisedly, but seriously and prayerfully, duly considering the purpose for which it is ordained.

It is ordained:

That husband and wife may give to each other life-long companionship, help, and comfort, both in prosperity and in adversity;

That God may hallow and direct the natural instincts and affections created by himself, and redeemed in Christ;

That children may be born and brought up in families in the knowledge of our Lord Jesus Christ to the glory of God;

That, marriage being thus held in honor, human society may stand upon firm foundations.

The Marriage

The minister says:

These two persons have come here to be made one in this holy estate. But if anyone here knows any just cause why they may not be married according to the discipline of the Church and the law of this land, let him now make it known, or else for ever hold his peace.

If no impediment is alleged, he says to the persons who are to be married:

I charge you both in the presence of God, that if either of you knows any reason why you may not be joined together in marriage, you do now confess it.

If no impediment is alleged, the man and woman may now garland each other; and the minister says:

Almighty and most merciful Father, without whose help we cannot do anything as we ought, we pray that, as thou hast brought these persons together by thy providence, thou wilt enrich them with thy grace, that they may enter into the marriage covenant as in thy sight, and truly keep the vows they are about to make; through Jesus Christ our Lord. **Amen.**

Then the minister says to the man:

_____, will you have this woman,
_____, to be your wife,
and cleave to her alone?

And the man answers:

I will.

The minister says to the woman:

_____, will you have this man,
_____, to be your husband,
and cleave to him alone?

And the woman answers:

I will.

If the woman is given in marriage by her parent or guardian, the minister says:

Who gives this woman to be married to this man?

And the parent or guardian puts the woman's right hand into the right hand of the man.

If the parent or guardian is not present, the minister says:

_____ and _____, give each other the right hand.

And the man says after the minister:

I, _____, Take you, _____, to be my wife, To have and to hold from this day forward; For better, for worse; For richer, for poorer; In sickness and in health; To love, cherish, and protect, till death us do part, According to God's holy law; And to this I give you my pledge.

They still hold hands, and the woman says after the minister:

I, _____, Take you, _____, to be my husband, To have and to hold from this day forward; For better, for worse; For richer, for poorer; In sickness and in health; To love, cherish, and obey, till death us do part, According to God's holy law; And to this I give you my pledge.

The minister says:

God has heard your vows, and we are witnesses.

The minister may bless the mangalasutra, ring, or rings, saying:

Bless this mangalasutra [ring], O merciful Lord, that he who gives it and she who wears it may ever be faithful one to the other, and continue together in love so long as they both shall live; through Jesus Christ our Lord. **Amen.**

The minister delivers the mangalasutra to the man, who puts it on the woman in the customary manner, and holds it. Or else the minister delivers the ring to the man, who puts it on the woman's finger, and holds it. The man then says after the minister:

This mangalasutra [ring] I give you in token of constant faith and abiding love. I honor you with my body, and all my worldly goods with you I share.

**If the woman gives a ring to the man, she puts it on his finger, and holds it, saying after the minister:*

This ring I give you in token of constant faith and abiding love. I honor you with my body, and all my worldly goods with you I share.

The minister declares:

As _____ and _____ have made their pledge to each other before God and before this congregation, I declare that they are now husband and wife, according to the law of this land and the ordinance of God; in the name of the Father, and of the Son, and of the Holy Spirit. **Amen.**

Whom therefore God has joined together, let not man put asunder.

The man and the woman kneel, while the congregation remains standing, and the minister says:

---

* Passages thus marked may be omitted at the discretion of the minister.

Most merciful and gracious God, our Father, of whom the whole family in heaven and earth is named: Send thy blessing upon _____ and _____, whom we bless in thy name; that, living faithfully together, they may surely perform and keep the vow and covenant between them made, and may ever remain in perfect love and peace together, and live according to thy law; through Jesus Christ our Lord. **Amen.**

God the Father, God the Son, God the Holy Spirit, bless, preserve, and keep you; the Lord mercifully look upon you with favor, and fill you with all spiritual benediction and grace: that you may so live together in this life that in the world to come you may have life everlasting. **Amen.**

The Prayers

A lyric or hymn is sung; or one or both of the following psalms may be said or sung. The man and woman go to the Lord's Table. If the ceremony of the Sapta-padi (Seven Steps) is observed, the people say or sing Psalm 67, pausing after each verse while the man and the woman take one step forward.

*Psalm 67

May God be gracious to us and bless us,
   and make his face to shine upon us,
that thy way may be known upon earth,
   thy saving power among all nations.
Let the peoples praise thee, O God;
   let all the peoples praise thee!

Let the nations be glad and sing for joy,
   for thou dost judge the peoples with equity
   and guide the nations upon earth.
Let the peoples praise thee, O God;
   let all the peoples praise thee!

The earth has yielded its increase;
   God, our God, has blessed us.
God has blessed us;
   Let all the ends of the earth fear him!

*Psalm 128

Blessed is everyone who fears the Lord,
   who walks in his ways!

You shall eat the fruit of the labor of your hands;
   you shall be happy, and it shall be well with you.

Your wife will be like a fruitful vine
   within your house;
your children will be like olive shoots
   around your table.
Lo, thus shall the man be blessed
   who fears the Lord.

The Lord bless you from Zion!
   May you see the prosperity of Jerusalem
   all the days of your life!
May you see your children's children!
   Peace be upon Israel!

After each psalm all say or sing:

Glory be to the Father: and to the Son, and to the Holy Spirit;
As it was in the beginning, is now, and ever shall be: world without end. **Amen.**

*A Bible or New Testament may then be placed in the hands of the newly married couple by the minister, with the words:

May the Word of God be a lamp to your feet and a light to your path.

The following passage of Scripture is read:

1 Corinthians 13:4–13

*A sermon may be preached.

Then the minister says:

Let us pray

Lord, have mercy upon us.
Christ, have mercy upon us.
Lord, have mercy upon us.

Our Father, who art in heaven, Hallowed be thy name. Thy kingdom come; Thy will be done; In earth as it is in heaven. Give us this day our daily bread; And forgive us our trespasses, As we forgive them that trespass against us; And lead us not into temptation, But deliver us from evil. For thine is the kingdom, The power and the glory, For ever and ever. Amen.

Lord, save thy servant and thy handmaid:
And let them put their trust in thee.

O Lord, send help from thy holy place:
And evermore defend them.

Be unto them a tower of strength:
From the face of their enemy.

O Lord, hear our prayer:
And let our cry come unto thee.

Almighty and everlasting Father, who has given to mankind the ordinance of marriage, and dost hallow it with thy blessing: Bless, we beseech thee, thy servants, _____ and _____, now joined together as husband and wife; and grant that, bearing one another's burdens, sharing one another's joys, and together fulfilling the duties of their home, they may ever be faithful to each other in love and obedience to thy word; through Jesus Christ our Lord. **Amen.**

O Lord and Savior Jesus Christ, who didst share at Nazareth the life of an earthly home: Reign, we beseech thee, in the home of these thy servants as Lord and King; give them grace that they may minister to others as thou didst minister to men, and grant that by deed and word they may be witnesses of thy saving love to those amongst whom they live; for thy holy name's sake, who livest and reignest with the Father and the Holy Spirit, one God, world without end. **Amen.**

The following prayer may be omitted if the woman is past child-bearing.

O Merciful Lord and heavenly Father, by whose gracious gift mankind is increased; Bestow, we beseech thee, upon these thy servants the heritage and gift of children, and grant that they may live together so long in godly love and honor, that they may see their children brought up in Christian faith and virtue, to thy praise and glory; through Jesus Christ our Lord. **Amen.**

O Almighty Lord, and everlasting God, vouchsafe, we beseech thee, to direct, sanctify, and govern, both our hearts and bodies in ways of thy laws, and in the works of thy commandments; that through thy most mighty protection, both here and ever, we may be preserved in body and soul; through our Lord and Savior Jesus Christ. **Amen.**

If the Lord's Supper follows, the service begins at the breaking of the Bread. Otherwise, the minister says:

The grace of our Lord Jesus Christ, and the love of God, and the fellowship of the Holy Spirit, be with you all. **Amen.**

A lyric or hymn may be sung while the register is being signed.

Source: *The Church of South India Book of Common Worship.* As Authorized by the Synod 1962. London: Oxford University Press, 1963.

Episcopal Wedding Service (1945)

THE FORM OF SOLEMNIZATION OF MATRIMONY

At the day and time appointed for Solemnization of Matrimony, the Persons to be married shall come into the body of the Church, or shall be ready in some proper house, with their friends and neighbors; and there standing together, the Man on the right hand, and the Woman on the left, the Minister shall say,

Dearly beloved, we are gathered together here in the sight of God, and in the face of this company, to join together this Man and this Woman in holy Matrimony; which is an honorable estate, instituted of God, signifying unto us the mystical union that is betwixt Christ and his Church: which holy estate Christ adorned and beautified with his presence and first miracle that he wrought in Cana of Galilee, and is commended of Saint Paul to be honorable among all men: and therefore is not by any to be entered into unadvisedly or lightly; but reverently, discreetly, advisedly, soberly, and in the fear of God. Into this holy estate these two persons present come now to be joined. If any man can show just cause, why they may not lawfully be joined together, let him now speak, or else hereafter for ever hold his peace.

And also speaking unto the Persons who are to be married, he shall say,

I require and charge you both, as ye will answer at the dreadful day of judgment when the secrets of all hearts shall be disclosed, that if either of you know any impediment, why ye may not be lawfully joined together in Matrimony, ye do now confess it. For be ye well assured, that if any persons are joined together otherwise than as God's Word doth allow, their marriage is not lawful.

The Minister, if he shall have reason to doubt of the lawfulness of the proposed Marriage, may demand sufficient surety for his indemnification: but if no impediment shall be alleged, or suspected, the minister shall say to the Man,

_____, wilt thou have this Woman to thy wedded wife, to live together after God's ordinance in the holy estate of Matrimony? Wilt thou love her, comfort her, honor, and keep her in sickness and in health; and, forsaking all others, keep thee only unto her, so long as ye both shall live?

The Man shall answer,

I will.

Then shall the Minister say unto the Woman,

_____, wilt thou have this Man to thy wedded husband, to live together after God's ordinance in the holy estate of Matrimony? Wilt thou love him, comfort him, honor, and keep him in sickness and in health; and, forsaking all others, keep thee only unto him, so long as ye both shall live?

The Woman shall answer,

I will.

Then shall the Minister say,

Who giveth this Woman to be married to this Man?

Then shall they give their troth to each other in this manner. The Minister, receiving the Woman at her father's or friend's hands, shall cause the Man with his right hand to take the Woman by her right hand, and to say after him as followeth.

I, _____, take thee, _____, to my wedded Wife, to have and to hold from this day forward, for better for worse, for richer for poorer, in sickness and in health, to love and to cherish, till death us do part, according to God's holy ordinance; and thereto I plight thee my troth.

Then shall they loose their hands; and the Woman with her right hand taking the Man by his right hand, shall likewise say after the Minister,

I, _____, take thee, _____, to my wedded Husband, to have and to hold from this day forward, for better for worse, for richer for poorer, in sickness and in health, to love and to cherish, till death us do part, according to God's holy ordinance; and thereto I plight thee my troth.

Then shall they again loose their hands; and the Man shall give unto the Woman a Ring on this wise: the Minister taking the Ring shall deliver it unto the Man, to put it upon the fourth finger of the Woman's left hand. And the Man holding the Ring there, and taught by the Minister, shall say,

With this Ring I thee wed: In the Name of the Father, and of the Son, and of the Holy Ghost. Amen.

And, before delivering the ring to the Man, the Minister may say as followeth.

Bless, O Lord, this Ring, that he who gives it and she who wears it may abide in thy peace, and continue in thy favor, unto their life's end; through Jesus Christ our Lord. Amen.

Then, the Man leaving the Ring upon the fourth finger of the Woman's left hand, the Minister shall say,

Let us pray.

Then shall the Minister and the People, still standing, say the Lord's Prayer.

Our Father, who art in heaven, Hallowed be thy Name. Thy kingdom come. Thy will be done, On earth as it is in heaven. Give us this day our daily bread. And forgive us our trespasses, As we forgive those who trespass against us. And lead us not into temptation, But deliver us from evil. For thine is the kingdom, and the power, and the glory, for ever and ever. Amen.

Then shall the Minister add,

O Eternal God, Creator and Preserver of all mankind, Giver of all spiritual grace, the Author of everlasting life; Send thy blessing upon these thy servants, this man and this woman, whom we bless in thy Name; that they, living faithfully together, may surely perform and keep the vow and covenant betwixt them made, (whereof this Ring given and received is a token and pledge,) and may ever remain in perfect love and peace together, and live according to thy laws; through Jesus Christ our Lord. **Amen.**

The Minister may add one or both of the following prayers.

O Almighty God, Creator of mankind, who only art the well-spring of life; Bestow upon these thy servants, if it be thy will, the gift and heritage of children; and grant that they may see their children brought up in thy faith and fear, to the honor and glory of thy Name; through Jesus Christ our Lord. **Amen.**

O God, who hast so consecrated the state of Matrimony that in it is represented the spiritual marriage and unity betwixt Christ and his Church; Look mercifully upon these thy servants, that they may love, honor, and cherish each other, and so live together in faithfulness and patience, in wisdom and true godliness, that their home may be a haven of blessing and of peace; through the same Jesus Christ our Lord, who liveth and reigneth with thee and the Holy Spirit ever, one God, world without end. **Amen.**

Then shall the Minister join their right hands together, and say,

Those whom God hath joined together let no man put asunder.

Then shall the Minister speak unto the company.

Forasmuch as _____ and _____ have consented the same before God and this company, and thereto have given and pledged their troth, each to the other, and have declared the same by giving and receiving a Ring, and by joining hands;

I pronounce that they are Man and Wife, In the Name of the Father, and of the Son, and of the Holy Ghost. Amen.

> *The Man and Wife kneeling, the Minister shall add this Blessing.*

God the Father, God the Son, God the Holy Ghost, bless, preserve, and keep you: the Lord mercifully with his favor look upon you, and fill you with all spiritual benediction and grace; that ye may so live together in this life, that in the world to come ye may have life everlasting. **Amen.**

Source: *The Book of Common Prayer*. Protestant Episcopal Church in the United States of America. New York: Church Hymnal Corp., 1945.

Episcopal Wedding Service (1979)

THE CELEBRATION AND BLESSING OF A MARRIAGE

At the time appointed, the persons to be married, with their witnesses, assemble in the church or some other appropriate place.

During the entrance, a hymn, psalm, or anthem may be sung, or instrumental music may be played.

Then the Celebrant, facing the people and the persons to be married, with the woman to the right and the man to the left, addresses the congregation and says

Dearly beloved: We have come together in the presence of God to witness and bless the joining together of this man and this woman in Holy Matrimony. The bond and covenant of marriage was established by God in creation, and our Lord Jesus Christ adorned this manner of life by his presence and first miracle at a wedding in Cana of Galilee. It signifies to us the mystery of the union between Christ and his Church, and Holy Scripture commends it to be honored among all people.

The union of husband and wife in heart, body, and mind is intended by God for their mutual joy; for the help and comfort given one another in prosperity and adversity; and, when it is God's will, for the procreation of children and their nurture in the knowledge and love of the Lord. Therefore marriage is not to be entered into unadvisedly or lightly, but reverently, deliberately, and in accordance with the purposes for which it was instituted by God.

Into this holy union _____ and _____ now come to be joined. If any of you can show just cause why they may not lawfully be married, speak now; or else for ever hold your peace.

Then the Celebrant says to the persons to be married

I require and charge you both, here in the presence of God, that if either of you know any reason why you may not be united in marriage lawfully, and in accordance with God's Word, you do now confess it.

The Declaration of Consent

The Celebrant says to the woman

_____, will you have this man to be your husband; to live together in the covenant of marriage? Will you love him, comfort him, honor and keep him, in sickness and in health; and, forsaking all others, be faithful to him as long as you both shall live?

The Woman answers

I will.

The Celebrant says to the man

_____, will you have this woman to be your wife; to live together in the covenant of marriage? Will you love her, comfort her, honor and keep her, in sickness and in health; and, forsaking all others, be faithful to her as long as you both shall live?

The Man answers

I will.

The Celebrant then addresss the congregation, saying

Will all of you witnessing these promises do all in your power to uphold these two persons in their marriage?

People

We will.

If there is to be a presentation or a giving in marriage, it takes place at this time. [The Celebrant shall say]

Who gives (presents) this woman to be married to this man?

or the following

Who presents this woman and this man to be married to each other?

To either question, the appropriate answer is "I do." If more than one person responds, they do so together.

A hymn, psalm, or anthem may follow.

The Ministry of the Word

The Celebrant then says to the people

The Lord be with you.

People

And also with you.

Celebrant

Let us pray.

O gracious and everliving God, you have created us male and female in your image: Look mercifully upon this man and this woman who come to you seeking your blessing, and assist them with your grace, that with true fidelity and steadfast love they may honor and keep the promises and vows they make; through Jesus Christ our Savior, who lives and reigns with you in the unity of the Holy Spirit, for ever and ever. **Amen.**

Then one or more of the following passages from Holy Scripture is read. If there is to be a Communion, a passage from the Gospel always concludes the Readings.

Genesis 1:26–28 (Male and female he created them)

Genesis 2:4–9, 15–24 (A man cleaves to his wife and they become one flesh)

Song of Solomon 2:10–13; 8:6–7 (Many waters cannot quench love)

Tobit 8:5b–8 (*New English Bible*) (That she and I may grow old together)

1 Corinthians 13:1–13 (Love is patient and kind)

Ephesians 3:14–19 (The Father from whom every family is named)

Ephesians 5:1–2, 21–33 (Walk in love, as Christ loved us)

Colossians 3:12–17 (Love which binds everything together in harmony)

1 John 4:7–16 (Let us love one another for love is of God)

Between Readings, a Psalm, hymn, or anthem may be sung or said. Appropriate Psalms are 67, 127, and 128.

When a passage from the Gospel is to be read, all stand, and the Deacon or Minister appointed says

The Holy Gospel of our Lord Jesus Christ according to _____.

People

Glory to you, Lord Christ.

Matthew 5:1–10 (The Beatitudes)

Matthew 5:13–16 (You are the light . . . Let your light so shine)

Matthew 7:21, 24–29 (Like a wise man who built his house upon the rock)

Mark 10:6–9, 13–16 (They are no longer two but one)

John 15:9–12 (Love one another as I have loved you)

After the Gospel, the Reader says

The Gospel of the Lord.

People

Praise to you, Lord Christ.

A homily or other response to the Readings may follow.

The Marriage

The man, facing the woman and taking her right hand in his, says

In the Name of God, I, _____, take you, _____, to be my wife, to have and to hold from this day forward, for better for worse, for richer for poorer, in sickness and in health, to love and to cherish, until we are parted by death. This is my solemn vow.

Then they loose their hands, and the woman, still facing the man, takes his right hand in hers, and says

In the Name of God, I, _____, take you, _____, to be my husband, to have and to hold from this day forward, for better for worse, for richer for poorer, in sickness and in health, to love and to cherish, until we are parted by death. This is my solemn vow.

They loose their hands.

The Priest may ask God's blessing on a ring or rings as follows

Bless, O Lord, *this ring* to be *a sign* of the vows by which this man and this woman have bound themselves to each other; through Jesus Christ our Lord. **Amen.**

The giver places the ring on the ring-finger of the other's hand and says

_____, I give you this ring as a symbol of my vow, and with all that I am, and all that I have, I honor you, in the Name of the Father, and of the Son, and of the Holy Spirit (*or* in the Name of God).

Then the Celebrant joins the right hands of husband and wife and says

Now that _____ and _____ have given themselves to each other by solemn vows, with the joining of hands and the giving and receiving of *a ring,* I pronounce that they are husband and wife, in the Name of the Father, and of the Son, and of the Holy Spirit.

Those whom God has joined together let no one put asunder.

People

Amen.

The Prayers

All standing, the Celebrant says

Let us pray together in the words our Savior taught us.

People and Celebrant

Our Father, who art in heaven,
    hallowed be thy Name,
    thy kingdom come,
    thy will be done,
        on earth as it is in heaven.
Give us this day our daily bread.
And forgive us our trespasses,
    as we forgive those
        who trespass against us.
And lead us not into temptation,
    but deliver us from evil.
For thine is the kingdom,
    and the power, and the glory,
for ever and ever. Amen.

or

Our Father in heaven,
    hallowed be your Name,
    your kingdom come,
    your will be done,
        on earth as in heaven.
Give us today our daily bread.
Forgive us our sins
    as we forgive those
        who sin against us.
Save us from the time of trial,
    and deliver us from evil.
For the kingdom, the power,
    and the glory are yours,
    now and for ever. Amen.

If Communion is to follow, the Lord's Prayer may be omitted here.

The Deacon or other person appointed reads the following prayers, to which the people respond, saying, Amen.

If there is not to be a Communion, one or more of the prayers may be omitted.

Let us pray.

Eternal God, creator and preserver of all life, author of salvation, and giver of all grace: Look with favor upon the world you have made, and for which your Son gave his life, and especially upon this man and this woman whom you make one flesh in Holy Matrimony. **Amen.**

Give them wisdom and devotion in the ordering of their common life, that each may be to the other a strength in need, a counselor in perplexity, a comfort in sorrow, and a companion in joy. **Amen.**

Grant that their wills may be so knit together in your will, and their spirits in your Spirit, that they may grow in love and peace with you and one another all the days of their life. **Amen.**

Give them grace, when they hurt each other, to recognize and acknowledge their fault, and to seek each other's forgiveness and yours. **Amen.**

Make their life together a sign of Christ's love to this sinful and broken world, that unity may overcome estrangement, forgiveness heal guilt, and joy conquer despair. **Amen.**

[Bestow on them, if it is your will, the gift and heritage of children, and the grace to bring them up to know you, to love you, and to serve you. **Amen.**]

Give them such fulfillment of their mutual affection that they may reach out in love and concern for others. **Amen.**

Grant that all married persons who have witnessed these vows may find their lives strengthened and their loyalties confirmed. **Amen.**

Grant that the bonds of our common humanity, by which all your children are united one to another, and the living to the dead, may be so transformed by your grace, that your will may be done on earth as it is in heaven; where, O Father, with your Son and the Holy Spirit, you live and reign in perfect unity, now and for ever. **Amen.**

The Blessing of the Marriage

The people remain standing. The husband and wife kneel, and the Priest says one of the following prayers

Most gracious God, we give you thanks for your tender love in sending Jesus Christ to come among us, to be born of a human mother, and to make the way of the cross to be the way of life. We thank you, also, for consecrating the union of man and woman in his Name. By the power of your Holy Spirit, pour out the abundance of your blessing upon this man and this woman. Defend them from every enemy. Lead them into all peace. Let their love for each other be a seal upon their hearts, a mantle about their shoulders, and a crown upon their foreheads. Bless them in their work and in their companionship; in their sleeping and in their waking; in their joys and in their sorrows; in their life and in their death. Finally, in your mercy, bring them to that table where your saints feast for ever in your heavenly home: through Jesus Christ our Lord, who with you and the Holy Spirit lives and reigns, one God, for ever and ever. **Amen.**

or this

O God, you have so consecrated the covenant of marriage that in it is represented the spiritual unity between Christ and his Church: Send therefore your blessing upon these your servants, that they may so love, honor, and cherish each other in faithfulness and patience, in wisdom and true godliness, that their home may be a haven of blessing and peace; through Jesus Christ our Lord, who lives and reigns with you and the Holy Spirit, one God, now and for ever. **Amen.**

The husband and wife still kneeling, the Priest adds this blessing

God the Father, God the Son, God the Holy Spirit, bless, preserve, and keep you; the Lord mercifully with his favor look upon you, and fill you with all spiritual benediction and grace; that you may faithfully live together in this life, and in the age to come have life everlasting. **Amen.**

The Peace

The Celebrant may say to the people

The peace of the Lord be always with you.

People

And also with you.

The newly married couple then greet each other, after which greetings may be exchanged throughout the congregation.

When Communion is not to follow, the wedding party leaves the church. A hymn, psalm, or anthem may be sung, or instrumental music may be played.

Source: *The Book of Common Prayer.* The Episcopal Church. New York: Seabury Press, 1979.

Evangelical Covenant Wedding Service

RITE OF MARRIAGE II

The wedding party may enter either during the processional music or during the singing of a congregational hymn. The woman will stand on the minister's right and the man on the left, with the other members of the wedding party on either side.

Address to the People

As a community of friends, we are gathered here in God's presence to witness the marriage of _____ and _____, and to ask God to bless them.

We are called to rejoice in their happiness, to help them when they have trouble, and to remember them in our prayers. Marriage, like our creation as men and women, owes its existence to God. It is his will and purpose that a husband and wife should love each other throughout their life (and that children born to them should enjoy the security of family and home).

Prayer

Eternal God, our Creator and Redeemer, as you gladdened the wedding at Cana in Galilee by the presence of your Son, so by your presence now bring your joy to this wedding. In favor look upon this couple and grant that they, rejoicing in all your gifts, may at length celebrate with Christ the Bridegroom, the marriage feast which has no end. Amen.

Charge to Couple

Speaking to the persons being married, the minister shall say:

_____ and _____, your marriage is intended to join you for life in a relationship so intimate and personal that it will change your whole being. God offers you the hope, and indeed the promise, of a love that is true and mature.

You have made it known that you want to be joined in Christian marriage, and no one has shown any valid reason why you may not. If either of you knows of any reason, you are now to declare it.

Declaration of Consent

Speaking to the groom, the minister will say:

_____, do you take _____ to be your wife, and do you commit yourself to her, to be responsible in the marriage relationship, to give yourself to her in love and work, to invite her fully into your being so that she can know who you are, to cherish her above all others and to respect her individuality, encouraging her to be herself and to grow in all that God intends?

The groom will answer:

Yes, I do.

Speaking to the bride, the minister will say:

_____, do you take _____ to be your husband, and do you commit yourself to him, to be responsible in the marriage relationship, to give yourself to him in love and work, to invite him fully into your being so that he can know who you are, to cherish him above all others and to respect his individuality, encouraging him to be himself and to grow in all that God intends?

The bride will answer:

Yes, I do.

Affirmation of Parents and Congregation

Inviting the parents to stand, the minister shall ask:

Do you as parents promise to pray for and support your children in the new relationship which they enter as husband and wife? If so, each say "I do."

I do.

Addressing the congregation, the minister will say:

All of you who witness these vows, will you do everything in your power to support and uphold these two persons in their marriage? Then say "We will!"

At this point, where space permits, the bride and groom and their two immediate attendants may move into the chancel.

Vows

The couple, taking each other's hands, shall say their vows:

I take you, _____, to be my wife from this day forward, to join with you and share all that is to come, and with the help of God I promise to be faithful to you as he gives us life together.

I take you, _____, to be my husband from this day forward, to join with you and share all that is to come, and with the help of God I promise to be faithful to you as he gives us life together.

or

I take you, _____, to be my wife. I promise before God and these witnesses to be your faithful husband, to share with you in plenty and in want, in joy and in sorrow, in sickness and in health, to forgive and strengthen you and to join with you so that together we may serve God and others as long as we both shall live.

I take you, _____, to be my husband. I promise before God and these witnesses to be your faithful wife, to share with you in plenty and in want, in joy and in sorrow, in sickness and in health, to forgive and strengthen you and to join with you so that together we may serve God and others as long as we both shall live.

Giving and Receiving of Rings

As the minister receives each ring in turn, it is appropriate to pray:

Bless, Lord, this ring that he/she who gives it and she/he who wears it may abide in your peace. Amen.

Giving the rings in turn, each shall say:

_____, I love you, and I give you this ring as a sign of my love and faithfulness.

Declaration of Marriage

Because _____ and _____ have made their vows with each other before God and all of us here, I declare them to be husband and wife in the name of God, Father, Son, and Holy Spirit. Amen.

Let no one divide those whom God has united.

Blessing

The Lord God who created our first parents and established them in marriage, establish and sustain you, that you may find delight in each other and grow in holy love until life's end. Amen.

Prayers of Thanksgiving and Intercession

O God, Creator and Father of us all, we thank you for the gift of life — and, in life, for the gift of marriage. We praise and thank you for all the joys that can come to men and women through marriage, and for the blessings of home and family.

Today, especially, we think of _____ and _____ as they begin their life together as husband and wife. With them we thank you for the joy they find in each other. Give them strength, Father, to keep the vows they have made and cherish the love they share, that they may be faithful and devoted. Help them to support each other with patience, understanding, and honesty. (Teach them to be wise and loving parents of any children they may have.) (We pray for their parents, that at this moment of parting they may rejoice in their children's happiness.)

Look with favor, God, on all our homes. Defend them from every evil that may threaten them, from outside or within. Let your Spirit so direct all of us that we may each look to the good of others in word and deed and grow in grace as we advance in years, through Jesus Christ our Lord. Amen.

Here the Lord's Prayer may be included:

Lord's Prayer

Our Father who art in heaven,
   hallowed be thy Name,
   thy kingdom come,
   thy will be done,
      on earth as it is in heaven.

Give us this day our daily bread.
And forgive us our debts
   as we forgive our debtors.
And lead us not into temptation,
   but deliver us from evil.
For thine is the kingdom, and the power,
   and the glory forever. Amen.

or

Our Father in heaven,
   hallowed be your Name,
   your kingdom come,
   your will be done,
      on earth as in heaven.
Give us today our daily bread.
Forgive us our sins
   as we forgive those who sin against us.
Save us from the time of trial
   and deliver us from evil.
For the kingdom, the power, and the glory
   are yours now and forever. Amen.

Benediction

The Lord bless you and keep you; the Lord make his face to shine upon you, and be gracious to you; the Lord lift up his countenance upon you, and give you peace. Amen.

or

Almighty God, Father, Son, and Holy Spirit, direct and keep you in his light and truth and love all the days of your life. Amen.

Following the service, the wedding party may leave the church during a hymn, suitable instrumental music, or in silence.

Source: *The Covenant Book of Worship*. The Evangelical Covenant Church of America. Chicago: Covenant Press, 1981.

Lutheran Wedding Service (1958)

ORDER FOR MARRIAGE

The Congregation shall stand for the Invocation.

The persons to be married having presented themselves at the entrance to the Chancel, before the Altar, the Man to the right of the Woman, the Minister shall say:

In the Name of the Father, and of the Son, and of the Holy Ghost. **Amen.**

Dearly Beloved: Forasmuch as Marriage is a holy estate, ordained of God, and to be held in honor by all, it becometh those who enter therein to weigh, with reverent minds, what the Word of God teacheth concerning it:

The Lord God said:

It is not good that the man should be alone; I will make him an help meet for him.

Our Lord Jesus Christ said:

Have ye not read that he which made them at the beginning made them male and female, and said, For this cause shall a man leave father and mother, and shall cleave to his wife, and they twain shall be one flesh? Wherefore, they are no more twain, but one flesh. What therefore God hath joined together, let not man put asunder.

Then shall be read one or both of the following Lections:

The Apostle Paul, speaking by the Holy Spirit, saith:

Husbands, love your wives, even as Christ also loved the Church, and gave himself for it. He that loveth his wife, loveth himself; for no man ever yet hated his own flesh, but nourisheth it, even as the Lord the Church. Wives, submit yourselves unto your own husbands, as unto the Lord; for the husband is the head of the wife, even as Christ is the Head of the Church.

The Apostle Peter, speaking by the Holy Spirit, saith:

Ye wives, let your adorning be the ornament of a meek and quiet spirit, which is, in the sight of God, of great price. Likewise, ye husbands, dwell with them according to knowledge, giving honor unto the wife as unto the weaker vessel and as being heirs together of the grace of life.

Then shall the Minister say:

And although, by reason of sin, many a cross hath been laid thereon, nevertheless our gracious Father in heaven doth not forsake his children in an estate so holy and acceptable to him, but is ever present with his abundant blessing.

If the Banns have not been published, then the Minister may say:

Into this holy estate this Man and this Woman come now to be united. If any one, therefore, can show just cause why they may not be lawfully joined together, let him now speak, or else forever hold his peace.

Then shall the Minister say to the Man:

_____, Wilt thou have this Woman to thy wedded wife, to live together after God's ordinance in the holy estate of Matrimony? Wilt thou love her, comfort her, honor and keep her in sickness and in health, and, forsaking all others, keep thee only unto her, so long as ye both shall live?

The Man shall say:

I will.

Then shall the Minister say to the Woman:

_____, Wilt thou have this Man to thy wedded husband, to live together after God's ordinance in the holy estate of Matrimony? Wilt thou love him, comfort him, honor and keep him in sickness and in health, and, forsaking all others, keep thee only unto him, so long as ye both shall live?

The Woman shall say:

I will.

If the Woman be given in Marriage, the Minister shall say:

Who giveth this Woman to be married to this Man?

The Minister shall then receive her at the hands of her father (or guardian or any friend), the Woman placing her right hand in the hand of the Minister. Then shall the Minister place the right hand of the Woman in the right hand of the Man. Then shall they loose their hands.

If the first part of the service has been conducted at the entrance to the Chancel, the Minister shall now precede the Man and Woman to the Altar.

The Man shall take the right hand of the Woman and say after the Minister:

I, _____, take thee, _____, to my wedded wife, to have and to hold from this day forward, for better for worse, for richer for poorer, in sickness and in health, to love and to cherish, till death us do part, according to God's holy ordinance; and thereto I plight thee my troth.

Then shall the Woman, in like manner, say after the Minister:

I, _____, take thee, _____, to my wedded husband, to have and to hold from this day forward, for better for worse, for richer for poorer, in sickness and in health, to love and to cherish, till death us do part, according to God's holy ordinance; and thereto I plight thee my troth.

Should a shorter form be desired, the following may be said:

[I, _____, take thee, _____, to my wedded (wife, *or,* husband), and plight thee my troth, till death us do part.]

If the wedding Ring be used, the minister shall now receive it and give it to the Man to put on the fourth finger of the Woman's left hand. Then shall the Man say, or if two rings be used, the Man and the Woman, in turn, shall say, after the Minister:

Receive this Ring as a token of wedded love and troth.

Then shall the Minister say:

Join your right hands.

Then shall the Minister lay his right hand upon their hands and say:

Forasmuch as _____ and _____ have consented together in holy wedlock, and have declared the same before God and in the presence of this company, I pronounce them Man and Wife: In the Name of the Father and of the Son and of the Holy Ghost. Amen.

What God hath joined together, let not man put asunder.

Then may they kneel, and the Minister shall bless them, saying:

The Lord, who created our first parents and sanctified their union in Marriage: Sanctify and bless you, that ye may please him both in body and soul, and live together in holy love until life's end. Amen.

Then shall the Minister say:

Let us pray.

Almighty and most merciful God, who has now united this Man and this Woman in the holy estate of Matrimony: Grant them grace to live therein according to thy holy Word; strengthen them in constant fidelity and true affection toward each other; sustain and defend them amidst all trials and temptations; and help them so pass through this world in faith toward thee, in communion with thy Holy church, and in loving service one of the other, that they may enjoy forever thy heavenly benediction; through Jesus Christ, thy Son, our Lord, who liveth and reigneth with thee and the Holy Ghost, one God, world without end. **Amen.**

The Minister may add one or both of the following prayers:

O Almighty God, Creator of mankind, who only art the well-spring of life: Bestow upon these thy servants, if it be thy will, the gift and heritage of children; and grant that they may see their children brought up in thy faith and fear, to the honor and glory of thy Name; through Jesus Christ, our Lord. **Amen.**

O God, who art our dwelling-place in all generations: Look with favor upon the homes of our land; enfold husband and wives, parents and children, in the bonds of thy pure love; and so bless our homes, that they may be a shelter for the defenseless, a bulwark for the tempted, a resting-place for the weary, and a foretaste of our eternal home in thee; through Jesus Christ our Lord. **Amen.**

Then shall all say:

Our Father, who art in heaven; Hallowed be Thy name; Thy kingdom come; Thy will be done on earth, as it is in heaven; Give us this day our daily bread; And forgive us our trespasses, as we forgive those who trespass against us; And lead us not into temptation; But deliver us from evil; For thine is the kingdom, and the power, and the glory, for ever and ever. Amen.

Then shall the Minister say the Benediction:

The Lord bless thee and keep thee. The Lord make his face shine upon thee, and be gracious unto thee. The Lord lift up his countenance upon thee, and give thee peace. **Amen.**

or

God Almighty send you his light and truth to keep you all the days of your life. The hand of God protect you; his holy Angels accompany you. God the Father, God the Son, and God the Holy Ghost, cause his grace to be mighty upon you. **Amen.**

Source: *Service Book and Hymnal.* Authorized by the Lutheran Churches cooperating in the Commission on the Liturgy and Hymnal (Music Edition). Minneapolis: Augsburg Publishing House, 1958.

Lutheran Wedding Service (1978)

MARRIAGE

Stand

1. The bride, groom, and wedding party stand in front of the minister. The parents may stand behind the couple.

P [Presiding minister]: The grace of our Lord Jesus Christ, the love of God, and the communion of the Holy Spirit be with you all.

C [Congregation]: And also with you.

A [Worship assistant]: Let us pray.

Eternal God, our creator and redeemer, as you gladdened the wedding at Cana in Galilee by the presence of your Son, so by his presence now bring your joy to this wedding. Look in favor upon _____ and _____ and grant that they, rejoicing in all your gifts, may at length celebrate with Christ the marriage feast which has no end.

C: Amen

Sit

2. One or more lessons from the Bible may be read. An address may follow. A hymn may be sung.

A: The Lord God in his goodness created us male and female, and by the gift of marriage founded human community in a joy that begins now and is brought to perfection in the life to come.

Because of sin, our age-old rebellion, the gladness of marriage can be overcast and the gift of the family can become a burden.

But because God, who established marriage, continues still to bless it with his abundant and ever-present support, we can be sustained in our weariness and have our joy restored.

P: _____ and _____, if it is your intention to share with each other your joys and sorrows and all that the years will bring, with your promises bind yourselves to each other as husband and wife.

Stand

3. The bride and groom face each other and join hands. Each, in turn, promises faithfulness to the other in these or similar words:

I take you, _____,
to be my wife/husband from this day forward,
to join with you and share all that is to come,
and I promise to be faithful to you
until death parts us.

4. The bride and groom exchange rings with these words:

I give you this ring as a sign of my love and faithfulness.

5. The bride and groom join hands, and the minister announces their marriage by saying:

P: _____ and _____, by their promises before God and in the presence of this congregation, have bound themselves to one another as husband and wife.

C: Blessed be the Father and the Son and the Holy Spirit now and forever.

P: Those whom God joined together let no one put asunder.

C: Amen

Sit

6: The bride and groom kneel.

P: The Lord God, who created our first parents and established them in marriage, establish and sustain you, that you may find delight in each other and grow in holy love until your life's end.

C: Amen

7. The parents may add their blessing with these or similar words; the wedding party may join them.

May you dwell in God's presence forever; may true and constant love preserve you.

8. The bride and groom stand.

Stand

A: Let us bless God for all the gifts in which we rejoice today.

P: Lord God, constant in mercy, great in faithfulness: With high praise we recall your acts of unfailing love for the human family, for the house of Israel, and for your people the Church.

We bless you for the joy which your servants, _____ and _____, have found in each other, and pray that you give to us such a sense of your constant love that we may employ all our strength in a life of praise of you, whose work alone holds true and endures forever.

C: Amen

A: Let us pray for _____ and _____ in their life together.

P: Faithful Lord, source of love, pour down your grace upon _____ and _____, that they may fulfill the vows they have made this day and reflect your steadfast love in their life-long faithfulness to each other. As members with them of the body of Christ, use us to support their life together; and from your great store of strength give them power and patience, affection and understanding,

courage, and love toward you, toward each other, and toward the world, that they may continue together in mutual growth according to your will in Jesus Christ our Lord.

C: Amen

Other intercessions may be offered.

A: Let us pray for all families throughout the world.

P: Gracious Father, you bless the family and renew your people. Enrich husbands and wives, parents and children more and more with your grace, that, strengthening and supporting each other, they may serve those in need and be a sign of the fulfillment of your perfect kingdom, where with your Son Jesus Christ, and the Holy Spirit, you live and reign, one God through all ages of ages.

C: Amen

9. When Holy Communion is celebrated, the service continues with the Peace.

10. When there is no Communion, the service continues with the Lord's Prayer.

C: Our Father in heaven,
    hallowed be your name,
    your kingdom come,
    your will be done,
        on earth as in heaven.
Give us today our daily bread.
Forgive us our sins
    as we forgive those
        who sin against us.
Save us from the time of trial
    and deliver us from evil.
For the kingdom, the power,
    and the glory are yours,
    now and forever. Amen

or

C: Our Father, who art in heaven,
    hallowed be thy name,
    thy kingdom come,
    thy will be done,
        on earth as it is in heaven.
Give us this day our daily bread;

and forgive us our trespasses,
   as we forgive those
      who trespass against us;
and lead us not into temptation,
   but deliver us from evil.
For thine is the kingdom,
   and the power, and the glory,
   forever and ever. Amen

P: Almighty God, Father, Son, and Holy Spirit, keep you in his light and truth and love now and forever.

C: Amen

Source: *Lutheran Book of Worship.* Lutheran Church in America, The American Lutheran Church, The Evangelical Lutheran Church of Canada, The Lutheran Church–Missouri Synod. Minneapolis: Augsburg Publishing House, 1978.

United Methodist Wedding Service (1964)

THE ORDER FOR THE SERVICE OF MARRIAGE

At the time appointed, the persons to be married, having been qualified according to the laws of the state and the standards of the Church, standing together facing the minister, the man at the minister's left hand and the woman at the right hand, the minister shall say,

Dearly beloved, we are gathered together here in the sight of God, and in the presence of these witnesses, to join together *this man and this woman* in holy matrimony: which is an honorable estate, instituted of God, and signifying unto us the mystical union which exists between Christ and his Church; which holy estate Christ adorned and beautified with his presence in Cana of Galilee. It is therefore not to be entered into unadvisedly, but reverently, discreetly, and in the fear of God. Into this holy estate these two persons come now to be joined. If any man can show just cause why they may not lawfully be joined together, let him now speak, or else hereafter forever hold his peace.

Addressing the persons to be married, the minister shall say:

I require and charge you both, as you stand in the presence of God, before whom the secrets of all hearts are disclosed, that, having duly considered the holy covenant you are about to make, you do now declare before this company your pledge of faith, each to the other. Be well assured that if these solemn vows are kept inviolate, as God's Word de- mands, and if steadfastly you endeavor to do the will of your heavenly Father, God will bless your marriage, will grant you fulfillment in it, and will establish your home in peace.

Then shall the minister say to the man, using his Christian name,

_____, wilt you have this woman to be thy wedded wife, to live together in the holy estate of matrimony? Wilt thou love her, comfort her, honor and keep her, in sickness and in health; and forsaking all other keep thee only unto her so long as ye both shall live?

The man shall answer,

I will.

Then shall the minister say to the woman, using her Christian name,

_____, wilt thou have this man to be thy wedded husband, to live together in the holy estate of matrimony? Wilt thou love him, comfort him, honor and keep him, in sickness and in health; and forsaking all other keep thee only unto him so long as ye both shall live?

The woman shall answer,

I will.

Then shall the minister say,

Who giveth this woman to be married to this man?

114

The father of the woman, or whoever gives her in marriage, shall answer,

I do.

Then the minister, receiving the hand of the woman from her father or other sponsor, shall cause the man with his right hand to take the woman by her right hand, and say after him,

I, _____, take thee, _____, to be my wedded wife, to have and to hold, from this day forward, for better, for worse, for richer, for poorer, in sickness and in health, to love and to cherish, till death us do part, according to God's holy ordinance; and thereto I pledge thee my faith.

Then shall they loose their hands; and the woman, with her right hand taking the man by his right hand, shall say after the minister,

I, _____, take thee, _____, to be my wedded husband, to have and to hold, from this day forward, for better, for worse, for richer, for poorer, in sickness and in health, to love and to cherish, till death us do part, according to God's holy ordinance; and thereto I pledge thee my faith.

Then they may give to each other rings, or the man may give to the woman a ring, in this wise: the minister taking the ring or rings, shall say,

The wedding ring is the outward and visible sign of an inward and spiritual grace, signifying to all the uniting of this man and this woman in holy matrimony, through the Church of Jesus Christ our Lord.

Then the minister may say,

Let us pray.
Bless, O Lord, the giving of these rings, that they who wear them may abide in thy peace, and continue in thy favor: through Jesus Christ our Lord. **Amen.**

Or, if there be but one ring, the minister may say,

Bless, O Lord, the giving of this ring, that he who gives it and she who wears it may abide forever in thy peace, and continue in thy favor; through Jesus Christ our Lord. **Amen.**

The minister shall then deliver the proper ring to the man to put upon the third finger of the woman's left hand. The man, holding the ring there, shall say after the minister,

In token and pledge of our constant faith and abiding love, with this ring I thee wed, in the name of the Father, and of the Son, and of the Holy Spirit. Amen.

Then, if there is a second ring, the minister shall deliver it to the woman to put upon the third finger of the man's left hand; and the woman, holding the ring there, shall say after the minister,

In token and pledge of our constant faith and abiding love, with this ring I thee wed, in the name of the Father, and of the Son, and of the Holy Spirit. Amen.

Then shall the minister join their right hands together and, with his hand on their united hands, shall say,

Forasmuch as _____ and _____ have consented together in holy wedlock, and have witnessed the same before God and this company, and thereto have pledged their faith each to the other and have declared the same by joining hands and by giving and receiving ring(s); I pronounce that they are husband and wife together, in the name of the Father, and of the Son, and of the Holy Spirit. Those whom God hath joined together let not man put asunder. **Amen.**

Then shall the minister say,

Let us pray.

Then shall the husband and wife kneel; the minister shall say,

O eternal God, creator and preserver of all mankind, giver of all spiritual grace, the author of everlasting life: Send thy blessings upon this man and this woman, whom we bless in thy name; that they may surely perform and keep the vow and covenant between them made, and may ever remain in perfect love and peace together, and live according to thy laws.

Look graciously upon them, that they may love, honor, and cherish each other, and so live together in faithfulness and patience, in wisdom and true godliness, that their home may be a haven of blessing and a place of peace; through Jesus Christ our Lord. **Amen.**

Then the husband and wife, still kneeling, shall join the minister and congregation in the Lord's Prayer, saying,

Our Father, who art in heaven, hallowed be thy name. Thy kingdom come, thy will be done on earth as it is in heaven. Give us this day our daily bread. And forgive us our trespasses, as we forgive those who trespass against us. And lead us not into temptation, but deliver us from evil. For thine is the kingdom, and the power, and the glory, forever. Amen.

Then the minister shall give this blessing:

God, the Father, the Son, and the Holy Spirit, bless, preserve, and keep you; the Lord graciously with his favor look upon you, and so fill you with all spiritual benediction and love that you may so live together in this life that in the world to come you may have life everlasting. **Amen.**

Source: *The Book of Worship of the United Methodist Church.* The Board of Publication of the Methodist Church, Inc. Nashville: Abingdon Press, 1964.

United Methodist Wedding Service (1985)

A SERVICE OF CHRISTIAN MARRIAGE

The Entrance

Gathering

While the people gather, instrumental or vocal music may be offered.

During the entrance of the wedding party, there may be instrumental music, or a hymn, a canticle, or an anthem.

Greeting

Minister to people:

Friends, we are gathered together in the sight of God to witness and to bless the joining together of _____ and _____ in Christian marriage. The covenant of marriage was established by God, who created us male and female for each other. With his presence and power, Jesus graced a wedding at Cana of Galilee and in his sacrificial love gave us the example for the love of husband and wife. _____ and _____ come to give themselves to one another in this holy covenant.

Declaration of Intention

Minister to the persons who are to marry:

I ask you now
in the presence of God and these people
to declare your intention
to enter into union with one another
through the grace of Jesus Christ,
who has called you into union with himself
through baptism.

Minister to woman:

_____, will you have _____
   to be your husband,
to live together in holy marriage?
Will you love him, comfort him,
honor and keep him
in sickness and in health,
and forsaking all others, be faithful to him
as long as you both shall live?

Woman:

I will.

Minister to the man:

_____, will you have _____
   to be your wife,
to live together in holy marriage?
Will you love her, comfort her, honor and keep her
in sickness and in health,
and forsaking all others, be faithful to her
as long as you both shall live?

Man:

I will.

The Response of the Families and People

Minister to people.

The marriage of
_____ and _____
unites two families
and creates a new one.
They ask for your blessing.

*Parents or other representatives of the families,
if present, may respond:*

We rejoice in your union,
and pray God's blessing upon you.

Minister to people:

Will all of you, by God's grace,
do everything in your power
to uphold and care for these two persons
in their marriage?

People:

We will.

Prayer

Minister to people:

The Lord be with you.

People:

And also with you.

Minister:

Let us pray.
God of all peoples:
You are the true light illumining everyone.
You show us the way, the truth, and the life.
You love us even when we are disobedient.
You sustain us with your Holy Spirit.
We rejoice in your life in the midst of our lives.
We praise you for your presence with us,
and especially in this act of solemn covenant.
Through Jesus Christ our Lord.
Amen.

Proclamation and Response

One or more Scripture lessons are read.

*A hymn, psalm, canticle, anthem, or other music may
be offered before or after readings.*

*A sermon or other witness to Christian marriage is
given.*

*Extemporaneous intercessory prayer may be offered, or
the following may be prayed by the minister or by all:*

Let us pray.
Eternal God,
creator and preserver of all life,
author of salvation, giver of all grace:
Bless and sanctify with your Holy Spirit
_____ and _____ who come
    now to join in marriage.
Grant that they may give their vows to each other
in the strength of your steadfast love.
Enable them to grow in love and peace
with you and with one another all their days,
that they may reach out
in concern and service to the world,
through Jesus Christ our Lord. **Amen.**

The Marriage

Exchange of Vows

*The woman and man face each other, joining hands.
Man to woman:*

In the name of God,
I, _____, take you, _____,
to be my wife,
to have and to hold
from this day forward,
for better for worse,
for richer for poorer,
in sickness and in health,
to love and to cherish,
until we are parted by death.
This is my solemn vow.

Woman to man:

In the name of God,
I, _____, take you, _____,
to be my husband,
to have and to hold
from this day forward,
for better for worse,
for richer for poorer,
in sickness and in health,
to love and to cherish,
until we are parted by death.
This is my solemn vow.

Blessing and Exchange of Rings

The minister may say:

These rings (*symbols*)
arc the outward and visible sign
of an inward and spiritual grace,
signifying to us the union
between Jesus Christ and his Church.

The minister may bless the giving of rings or other symbols of the marriage.

Bless, O Lord, the giving of these rings (*symbols*),
that they who wear them may live in your peace,
and continue in your favor all the days of their life,
through Jesus Christ our Lord. **Amen.**

The giver(s) may say to the recipient(s):

_____, I give you this ring (*symbol*)
as a sign of my vow,
and with all that I am,
and all that I have,
I honor you
in the name of the Father,
and of the Son,
and of the Holy Spirit.

Declaration of Marriage

The wife and husband join hands. The minister may place a hand on, or wrap a stole around, their joined hands.

Minister to husband and wife:

You have declared your consent and vows
before God and this congregation.
May God confirm your covenant
and fill you both with grace.

Minister to people:

Now that _____ and _____
have given themselves to each other by solemn vows,
with the joining of hands,
and the giving and receiving of *rings,*
I announce to you that they are husband and wife
in the name of the Father, and of the Son,
and of the Holy Spirit.
Those whom God has joined together,
let no one put asunder.

People:

Amen.

A doxology or other hymn may be sung.

Intercessions may be offered by the Church and for the world.

Blessing of the Marriage

The husband and wife may kneel, as the minister prays:

O God,
you have so consecrated the
covenant of Christian marriage
that in it is represented
the covenant between Christ and his Church.
Send therefore your blessing upon _____
and _____,
that they may surely keep their marriage covenant
and so grow in love and godliness together,
that their home may be a haven
of blessing and peace,
through Jesus Christ our Lord.

Amen.

If Holy Communion is not to be celebrated, the service continues with the Lord's Prayer and concludes with the Sending Forth.

Thanksgiving and Communion

Taking the Bread and Cup

> *Minister to people:*

Let us offer ourselves and our gifts to God.

> *Here the husband and wife or representatives of the con-gregation may bring the bread and wine to the Lord's table. The minister takes them and prepares them for the meal.*

The Great Thanksgiving

The Lord be with you.
And also with you.

Lift up your hearts.
We lift them to the Lord.

Let us give thanks to the Lord our God.
It is right to give our thanks and praise.

It is right, and a good and joyful thing,
always and everywhere to give thanks to you,
Father Almighty, Creator of heaven and earth.
You formed us in your image,
male and female you created us.
You gave us the gift of marriage,
that we might fulfill one another.
And so,
with your people on earth and all the company of
heaven
we praise your name and join their unending hymn:

**Holy, holy, holy Lord, God of power and might,
heaven and earth are full of your glory.
Hosanna in the highest.
Blessed is he who comes in the name of the Lord.
Hosanna in the highest.**

Holy are you, and blessed is your Son Jesus Christ.
By the baptism
of his suffering, death, and resurrection
you gave birth to your Church,
delivered us from slavery to sin and death,
and made with us a new covenant
by water and the Spirit
from which flows the covenant love
of husband and wife.

On the night in which he gave himself up for us
he took bread, gave thanks to you, broke the bread,
gave it to his disciples, and said:
"Take, eat; this is my body which is given for you.
Do this in remembrance of me."

When the supper was over he took the cup,
gave thanks to you, gave it to his disciples, and said:
"Drink from this, all of you;
this is my blood of the new covenant,
poured out for you and for many
for the forgiveness of sins.
Do this, as often as you drink it,
in remembrance of me."

And so,
in remembrance of these your mighty acts
in Jesus Christ,
we offer ourselves in praise and thanksgiving
as a holy and living sacrifice,
in union with Christ's offering for us,
as we proclaim the mystery of faith.

**Christ has died, Christ is risen, Christ will come
again.**

Pour out your Holy Spirit on us, gathered here,
and on these gifts of bread and wine.
Make them be for us the body and blood of Christ,
that we may be for the world the body of Christ,
redeemed by his blood.

By the same Spirit bless
_____ and _____,
that their love for each other
may reflect the love of Christ for us
and grow from strength to strength
as they faithfully serve you in the world.
Finally, by your grace,
bring them and all of us to that table
where your saints feast forever
in your heavenly home.

Through your Son Jesus Christ,
with the Holy Spirit in your holy Church,
all honor and glory is yours, Almighty Father,
now and for ever.

Amen.

And now, with the confidence of children of God, let us pray:

All pray the Lord's Prayer.

Breaking the Bread

The minister breaks the bread and then lifts the cup, in silence or with appropriate words.

Giving the Bread and Cup

The bread and wine are given to the people, with these or other words being exchanged:

The body of Christ, given for you. **Amen.**
The blood of Christ, given for you. **Amen.**

Sending Forth

Here may be a hymn or Psalm 128.

Dismissal with Blessing

God the Eternal keep you in love with each other, so that the peace of Christ may abide in your home. Go to serve God and your neighbor in all that you do.

Bear witness to the love of God in this world so that those to whom love is a stranger will find in you generous friends. The grace of the Lord Jesus Christ, and the love of God, and the communion of the Holy Spirit be with you all.

Amen.

The Peace

The peace of the Lord be with you always.
And also with you.

The couple and minister(s) may greet each other, after which greetings may be exchanged throughout the congregation.

Going Forth

A hymn may be sung or instrumental music played as the couple, the wedding party, and the people leave.

Source: *The Book of Services*. Nashville: United Methodist Publishing House, 1985.

Moravian Wedding Service

SOLEMNIZATION OF MATRIMONY

The persons to be married shall stand before the minister with their witnesses, the man standing at the right hand of the woman. Then the minister shall say:

Dearly beloved, we are here assembled, in the presence of God and these witnesses, to join together this man, _____, and this woman, _____, in holy marriage, which is blessed by our Lord Jesus Christ, governed by God's commandments, and is to be held in honor among all men. Therefore it is not to be entered into unadvisedly or lightly, but reverently, discreetly, and in the fear of God.

In Holy Scripture we are taught:

That marriage was instituted by God Himself, and is therefore an holy estate; that, according to the ordinance of God, a man and his wife shall be one flesh; that, under the New Covenant, the married state hath been sanctified to be an emblem of Christ and His Church; that the husband, as the head of the wife, should love her, even as Christ also loveth the Church; and that the wife be subject to her own husband in the Lord, as the Church is subject unto Christ; that, in consequence, Christians thus united together should love one another, as one in the Lord, be faithful one to the other, bear with each other's infirmities and weaknesses, cherish each other in joy and sorrow, pray for and encourage each other in all things, and live together as heirs of the grace of life.

Into this holy estate these two persons come now to be joined. If any man can show just cause why they may not lawfully be joined together, according to the Word of God and the laws of this State, let him now speak, or else forever hold his peace.

If no question is raised as to the lawfulness of the proposed marriage, the minister shall say to the man, addressing him by his Christian name:

_____, will you have this woman to be your wife, to live together in the holy bond of marriage? Will you love her, honor her, and care for her, under all conditions and circumstances of life, and through the grace of God approve yourself a faithful Christian husband to her so long as you both shall live? If this is your desire then answer and say, "I will."

The man shall answer:

I will.

The minister shall say to the woman, addressing her by her Christian name:

_____, will you have this man to be your husband, to live together in the holy bond of marriage? Will you love him, honor him, and care for him, under all conditions and circumstances of life, and through the grace of God approve yourself a faithful Christian wife to him so long as you both shall live? If this is your desire then answer and say, "I will."

The woman shall answer:

I will.

The minister shall cause the man with his right hand to take the woman by her right hand and to say after him as follows:

I, _____, take you, _____, to be my wedded wife; and I do promise and covenant to be your loving and faithful husband; for better, for worse; for richer, for poorer; in sickness and in health; so long as we both shall live.

They shall release hands; and the woman, with her right hand taking the man by his right hand, shall likewise say after the minister:

I, _____, take you, _____, to be my wedded husband; and I do promise and covenant to be your loving and faithful wife; for better, for worse; for richer, for poorer; in sickness and in health; so long as we both shall live.

If a ring is used, the man shall here give the ring to the woman, which the minister taking from her shall deliver again to the man and say:

Take this ring and place it upon the finger of this woman and say:

The man shall repeat after the minister:

This ring I give to you, in token and pledge of our constant faith and abiding love.

If a second ring is used, a similar order shall be followed, the woman saying the same words after the minister.

Let us pray.

Most merciful and gracious God, of Whom the whole family in heaven and earth is named, we thank Thee for the love with which Thou dost bind kindred souls together, and especially for the institution of marriage, the tenderness of its ties, the honor of its estate, and the sacredness of its obligations. Look with favor upon these Thy servants; sanctify and bless their union; grant them grace to fulfill, with pure and steadfast affection, the vow and covenant made between them. Guide them together, we pray, in the way of righteousness and peace, that, loving and serving Thee, with one heart and mind, all the days of their life, they may be abundantly enriched by Thy grace. Vouchsafe unto them the guidance of Thy Holy Spirit, and teach them to do that which is well pleasing in Thy sight, through Jesus Christ, our Lord. Amen.

The minister shall join their right hands and say:

In the name of God the Father, the Son, and the Holy Spirit, I now join you together to live within the bonds of holy marriage, as husband and wife. What therefore God has joined together, let no man put asunder. Receive the blessing of the Lord.

The man and the woman shall kneel.

The Lord bless you, and keep you;

The Lord make His face shine upon you, and be gracious unto you;

The Lord lift up His countenance upon you, and give you peace:

In the Name of Jesus. Amen.

Source: *Hymnal and Liturgies of the Moravian Church*. Bethlehem, Pa.: Department of Publications, Moravian Church, Northern Province, 1969. A new Moravian hymnal will be published about 1995.

Presbyterian Wedding Service (1946)

ORDER FOR THE SOLEMNIZATION
OF MARRIAGE

The Persons to be married shall present themselves before the Minister, the Man standing at the right hand of the Woman. Then, all present reverently standing, the Minister shall say:

Dearly Beloved, we are assembled here in the presence of God, to join this Man and this Woman in holy marriage; which is instituted by God, regulated by His commandments, blessed by our Lord Jesus Christ, and to be held in honor among all men. Let us therefore reverently remember that God has established and sanctified marriage, for the welfare and happiness of mankind. Our Savior has declared that a man shall leave his father and mother and cleave unto his wife. By His apostles, He has instructed those who enter into this relation to cherish a mutual esteem and love; to bear with each other's infirmities and weaknesses; to comfort each other in sickness, trouble, and sorrow; in honesty and industry to provide for each other, and for their household, in temporal things; to pray for and encourage each other in the things which pertain to God; and to live together as the heirs of the grace of life.

Forasmuch as these two Persons have come hither to be made one in this holy estate, if there be any here present who knows any just cause why they may not lawfully be joined in marriage, I require him now to make it known, or ever after to hold his peace.

Then, speaking unto the Persons who are to be married, the Minister shall say:

I charge you both, before the great God, the Searcher of all hearts, that if either of you know any reason why ye may not lawfully be joined together in marriage, ye do now confess it. For be ye well assured that if any persons are joined together otherwise than as God's Word allows, their union is not blessed by Him.

Then, if no impediment appear, the Minister shall say:

Let us pray.

Almighty and ever-blessed God, whose presence is the happiness of every condition, and whose favor hallows every relation: We beseech Thee to be present and favorable unto these Thy servants, that they may be truly joined in the honorable estate of marriage, in the covenant of their God. As Thou hast brought them together by Thy providence, sanctify them by Thy Spirit, giving them a new frame of heart fit for their new estate; and enrich them with all grace, whereby they may enjoy the comforts, undergo the cares, endure the trials, and perform the duties of life together as becometh Christians, under Thy heavenly guidance and protection; through our Lord Jesus Christ. **Amen.**

Then the Minister, calling the Man by his Christian name, shall say:

_____, wilt thou have this Woman to be thy wife, and wilt thou pledge thy troth to her, in all love and honor, in all duty and service, in all faith and tenderness, to live with her, and cherish her, according to the ordinance of God, in the holy bond of marriage?

The Man shall answer:

I will.

Then the Minister, calling the Woman by her Christian name, shall say:

_____, wilt thou have this Man to be thy husband, and wilt thou pledge thy troth to him, in all love and honor, in all duty and service, in all faith and tenderness, to live with him, and cherish him, according to the ordinance of God, in the holy bond of marriage?

The Woman shall answer:

I will.

Then the Minister may say:

Who giveth this Woman to be married to this Man?

Then the Father, or Guardian, or Friend, of the Woman shall put her right hand in the hand of the minister, who shall cause the Man with his right hand to take the Woman by her right hand and say after the Minister as follows:

I, _____, take thee, _____; To be my wedded wife; And I do promise and covenant; Before God and these witnesses; To be thy loving and faithful husband; In plenty and in want; In joy and in sorrow; In sickness and in health; As long as we both shall live.

Then shall they loose their hands; and the Woman, with her right hand taking the man by his right hand, shall likewise say after the Minister:

I, _____, take thee, _____; To be my wedded husband; And I do promise and covenant; Before God and these witnesses; To be thy loving and faithful wife; In plenty and in want; In joy and in sorrow; In sickness and in health; As long as we both shall live.

Then if a ring be provided, it shall be given to the Minister, who shall return it to the Man, who shall then put it upon the fourth finger of the Woman's left hand, saying after the Minister:

This ring I give thee; In token and pledge; Of our constant faith; and Abiding love.

or

With this ring I thee wed; In the name of the Father; And the Son; And of the Holy Spirit. Amen.

Before giving the ring, the Minister may say:

Bless, O Lord, this ring, that he who gives it and she who wears it may abide in Thy peace, and continue in Thy favor, unto their life's end; through Jesus Christ our Lord. **Amen.**

If a second ring be provided, a similar order shall be followed, the Woman saying the same words after the Minister.

Then the Minister shall say:

Let us pray.

Most merciful and gracious God, of whom the whole family in heaven and earth is named: Bestow upon these Thy servants the seal of Thine approval, and Thy Fatherly benediction; granting unto them grace to fulfill, with pure and steadfast affection, the vow and covenant between them made. Guide them together, we beseech Thee, in the way of righteousness and peace, that, loving and serving Thee, with one heart and mind, all the days of their life, they may be abundantly enriched with the token of Thine everlasting favor, in Jesus Christ our Lord. **Amen.**

Then the Minister and People shall say:

Our Father, who art in heaven; Hallowed be Thy name. Thy kingdom come. Thy will be done; On earth as it is in heaven. Give us this day our daily bread. And forgive us our debts; As we forgive our debtors. And lead us not into temptation; But deliver us from evil; for Thine is the kingdom, and the power, and the glory, for ever. Amen.

Then shall the Minister say unto all who are present:

By the authority committed unto me as a Minister of the Church of Christ, I declare that _____ and _____ are now Husband and Wife, according to the ordinance of God, and the law of the State; in the name of the Father, and of the Son, and of the Holy Spirit. Amen.

Then, causing the Husband and wife to join their right hands, the Minister shall say:

Whom therefore God hath joined together, let no man put asunder.

It is fitting that the Bride and Groom kneel to receive the Benediction:

The Lord bless you, and keep you: the Lord make His face to shine upon you, and be gracious unto you: the Lord lift up His countenance upon you, and give you peace: both now and in the life everlasting. **Amen.**

or

God the Father, God the Son, God the Holy Spirit, bless, preserve, and keep you, the Lord mercifully with His favor look upon you, and fill you with all spiritual benediction and grace; that ye may so live together in this life that in the world to come ye may have life everlasting. **Amen.**

Source: *The Book of Common Worship*. The Board of Christian Education of the Presbyterian Church in the United States of America. Philadelphia: Westminster Press, 1946.

Presbyterian Wedding Service (1970)

THE MARRIAGE SERVICE

The man and the woman to be married may be seated together facing the Lord's table, with their families, friends, and members of the congregation seated with them.

When the people have assembled, let the minister say:

Let us worship God.

There was a marriage at Cana in Galilee; Jesus was invited to the marriage, with his disciples.

Friends: Marriage is established by God. In marriage a man and a woman willingly bind themselves together in love, and become one even as Christ is one with the church, his body.

Let marriage be held in honor among all.

All may join in a hymn of praise and the following prayer:

Let us confess our sin before God.

Almighty God, our Father: you created us for life together. We confess that we have turned from your will. We have not loved one another as you commanded. We have been quick to claim our own rights and careless of the rights of others. We have taken much and given little. Forgive our disobedience, O God, and strengthen us in love, so that we may serve you as a faithful people, and live together in your joy; through Jesus Christ our Lord. Amen.

The minister shall declare God's mercy, saying:

Hear and believe the good news of the gospel.

Nothing can separate us from the love of God in Christ Jesus our Lord!

In Jesus Christ, we are forgiven.

The people may stand to sing a doxology, or some other appropriate response to the good mercy of God.

The minister may offer a Prayer for Illumination.

Before the reading of the Old Testament lesson, the minister shall say:

The lesson is . . .

Listen for the word of God.

The Gloria Patri, or some other response, may be sung.

Before the reading of the New Testament lesson, the minister shall say:

The lesson is . . .

Listen for the word of God.

The minister may deliver a brief Sermon on the lessons from the Scripture, concluding with an Ascription of Praise.

Then let the minister address the man and woman saying:

_____ and _____, you have come together according to God's wonderful plan for creation. Now, before these people, say your vows to each other.

Let the man and the woman stand before the people, facing each other. Then, the minister shall say:

Be subject to one another out of reverence for Christ.

The man shall say to the woman:

_____, I promise with God's help to be your faithful husband, to love and serve you as Christ commands, as long as we both shall live.

The woman shall say to the man:

_____, I promise with God's help to be your faithful wife, to love and serve you as Christ commands, as long as we both shall live.

A ring, or rings, may be given, with the following words:

I give you this ring as a sign of my promise.

The minister shall address the man and the woman, saying:

As God's picked representatives of the new humanity, purified and beloved of God himself, be merciful in action, kindly in heart, humble in mind. Accept life, and be most patient and tolerant with one another. Forgive as freely as the Lord has forgiven you. And, above everything else, be truly loving. Let the peace of Christ rule in your hearts, remembering that as members of the one body you are called to live in harmony, and never forget to be thankful for what God has done for you.

or

Love is slow to lose patience — it looks for a way of being constructive. It is not possessive; it is neither anxious to impress nor does it cherish inflated ideas of its own importance. Love has good manners and does not pursue selfish advantage. It is not touchy. It does not keep account of evil or gloat over the wickedness of other people. On the contrary, it is glad with all good men when truth prevails. Love knows no limit to its endurance, no end to its trust, no fading of its hope; it can outlast anything. It still stands when all else has fallen.

The minister shall call the people to prayer, saying:

Praise the Lord.

The Lord's name be praised.

Lift up your hearts.

We lift them to the Lord.

Let us pray.

Eternal God: without your grace no promise is sure. Strengthen _____ and _____ with the gift of your Spirit, so they may fulfill the vows they have taken. Keep them faithful to each other and to you. Fill them with such love and joy that they may build a home where no one is a stranger. And guide them by your word to serve you all the days of their lives; through Jesus Christ our Lord, to whom be honor and glory forever and ever. **Amen.**

The Lord's Prayer shall be said.

Then, the man and the woman having joined hands, the minister shall say:

_____ and _____, you are now husband and wife according to the witness of the holy catholic church, and the law of the state. Become one. Fulfill your promises. Love and serve the Lord.

What God has united, man must not divide.

Here may be sung a hymn of thanksgiving. Then, let the people be dismissed:

Glory be to him who can keep you from falling and bring you safe to his glorious presence, innocent and happy. To God, the only God, who saves us through Jesus Christ our Lord, be the glory, majesty, authority, and power, which he had before time began, now and forever. **Amen.**

or

The grace of the Lord Jesus Christ, the love of God, and the fellowship of the Holy Spirit, be with you all. **Amen.**

Source: *The Worshipbook: Services and Hymns.* The Joint Committee on Worship for Cumberland Presbyterian Church, Presbyterian Church in the United States, and The United Presbyterian Church in the United States of America. Philadelphia: Westminster Press, 1970, 1972.

Presbyterian Wedding Service (1986 Rite I)

CHRISTIAN MARRIAGE: A SERVICE FOR GENERAL USE

Entrance

As the people gather, music appropriate to the praise of God may be offered. At the appointed time the bride, groom, and other members of the wedding party present themselves and stand before the minister. The families may stand with the couple. A psalm, hymn, spiritual, or anthem may be sung, or instrumental music may be played, as the wedding party enters.

Sentences of Scripture

Either before or after the entrance, the people are called to worship with these or other words from Scripture:

God is love, and those who abide in love
abide in God, and God abides in them.
   (1 John 4:16)

   or

This is the day the Lord has made.
Let us rejoice and be glad in it. (Psalm 118:24)

Statement on the Gift of Marriage

The minister shall say:

We have gathered in the presence of God
to give thanks for the gift of marriage,
to witness the joining together of _____
   and _____,
to surround them with our prayers,
and to ask God's blessing upon them,
so that they may be strengthened for their life together
and nurtured in their love of God.

God created us male and female,
and gave us marriage
so that husband and wife may help and comfort each
   other,
living faithfully together in plenty and in want,
in joy and sorrow,
in sickness and in health,
throughout all their days.

God gave us marriage
for the full expression of the love between a man and
   a woman.
In marriage, a woman and a man belong to each
   other,
and with affection and tenderness
freely give themselves to each other.

God gave us marriage
for the well-being of human society,
for the ordering of family life,
and for the birth and nurture of children.

God gave us marriage as a holy mystery
in which a man and a woman are joined together
and become one,
just as Christ is one with the church.

In marriage, husband and wife are called to a new
   way of life,
created, ordered, and blessed by God.
This way of life must not be entered into carelessly,
or from selfish motives,
but responsibly, and prayerfully.

We rejoice that marriage is given by God,
blessed by our Lord Jesus Christ,
and sustained by the Holy Spirit.
Therefore, let marriage be held in honor among all.

Prayer

The minister says:

Let us pray.

Gracious God,
you are always faithful in your love for us.
Look mercifully upon
_____ and _____,
who have come seeking your blessing.
Let your Holy Spirit rest upon them
so that with steadfast love
they may honor the promises they make this day,
through Jesus Christ our Savior.

Amen.

Declaration of Intent

The minister addresses the bride and groom individually:

_____, having heard how God has cre-
   ated, ordered, and blessed the covenant of marriage,
do you affirm your desire and intention
to enter this covenant?

Answer:

I do.

Or if both are baptized, the following may be used.

_____, in your baptism
you have been called to union with Christ and the
   church.

Do you intend to honor this calling
through the covenant of marriage?

Answer:

I do.

Affirmations of the Families

The minister may address the families of the bride and groom:

(*Family members*) _____,
do you give your blessing to _____ and
_____,
and promise to do everything in your power to
   uphold them in their marriage?

Answer:

We (I) give our (my) blessing
and promise our (my) loving support.

or

We (I) do.

The families may be seated.

Affirmation of the Congregation

The minister may then address the congregation. The congregation may stand.

Will all of you witnessing these vows
do everything in your power to uphold
_____ and _____
in their marriage?

Answer:

We will.

A psalm, hymn, spiritual, or anthem may be sung.

Scripture and Sermon

The following, or a similar prayer for illumination, may be said.

God of mercy,
you have never broken your covenant with us,
and you free us to live together
in the power of your faithful love.
Amid all the changing words of our generation,
may we hear your eternal Word that does not change.
Then may we respond to your gracious promises
with faithful and obedient lives;
through our Lord Jesus Christ.

Amen.

Scripture shall be read. A brief sermon may follow. A psalm, hymn, spiritual, or other music may be used.

Vows

The minister addresses the couple:

_____ and _____,
since it is your intention to marry,
join your right hands,
and with your promises
bind yourselves to each other as husband and wife.

The bride and groom face each other and join right hands. Then, they shall say their vows to each other, in turn.

The man says:

I, _____, take you, _____,
to be my wife;
and I promise,
before God and these witnesses,
to be your loving and faithful husband;
in plenty and in want;
in joy and in sorrow;
in sickness and in health;
as long as we both shall live.

or

The man says:

Before God and these witnesses,
I, _____, take you, _____,
to be my wife,
and I promise to love you,
and to be faithful to you
as long as we both shall live.

The woman says:

I, _____, take you, _____,
to be my husband;
and I promise,
before God and these witnesses,
to be your loving and faithful wife;
in plenty and in want;
in joy and in sorrow;
in sickness and in health;
as long as we both shall live.

or

The woman says:

Before God and these witnesses,
I, _____, take you, _____,
to be my husband,
and I promise to love you,
and to be faithful to you,
as long as we both shall live.

Exchange of Rings (or Other Symbols)

If rings are to be exchanged, the minister says to the couple:

What do you bring as a sign of your promise?

When the rings are presented the minister may say the following prayer.

By your blessing, O God,
may these rings be to _____ and

_____
symbols of unending love and faithfulness,
reminding them of the covenant they have made this
   day,
through Jesus Christ our Lord.

Amen.

The bride and groom shall exchange rings using these or other appropriate words.

The one giving the ring says:

_____, I give you this ring
as a sign of our covenant,

in the name of the Father,
and of the Son,
and of the Holy Spirit.

or

As each ring is given, the one giving the ring says:

This ring I give you,
as a sign of our constant faith
and abiding love,
in the name of the Father,
and of the Son,
and of the Holy Spirit.

The one receiving the ring says:

I receive this ring,
as a sign of our covenant
in the name of the Father,
and of the Son,
and of the Holy Spirit.

Prayer

The couple may kneel.

One of the following prayers, or a similar prayer, is said:

Let us pray:

Eternal God,
creator and preserver of all life,
author of salvation
and giver of all grace:
look with favor upon the world you have made and
    redeemed,
and especially upon _____ and

_____.

Give them wisdom and devotion in their common
    life,
that each may be to the other
a strength in need,
a comfort in sorrow,
a counselor in perplexity,
and a companion in joy.

Grant that their wills may be so knit together in your
    will,
and their spirits in your Spirit,

that they may grow in love and peace
with you and each other
all the days of their life.

Give them courage,
when they hurt each other,
to recognize and confess their fault,
and the grace to seek your forgiveness,
and to forgive each other.

Make their life together
a sign of Christ's love to this sinful and broken world,
that unity may overcome estrangement,
forgiveness heal guilt,
and joy conquer despair.

Give them such fulfillment of their mutual love
that they may reach out in concern for others.

[Give to them, if it is your will,
the gift of children,
and the wisdom to bring them up
to know you, to love you,
and to serve you.]

Grant that all who have witnessed these vows today
may find their lives strengthened,
and that all who are married
may depart with their own promises renewed.

Enrich with your grace
all husbands and wives, parents and children,
that, loving and supporting one another,
they may serve those in need
and be a sign of your kingdom.

Grant that the bonds of our common humanity,
by which all your children are united one to another,
may be so transformed by your Spirit
that your peace and justice may fill the earth,
through Jesus Christ our Lord.

Amen.

or

Eternal God,
without your grace no promise is sure.
Strengthen _____ and _____
with patience, kindness, gentleness,
and all other gifts of your Spirit,
so that they may fulfill the vows they have made.

Keep them faithful to each other and to you.
Fill them with such love and joy
that they may build a home of peace and welcome.
Guide them by your word
to serve you all their days.

Enable us all, O God,
in each of our homes and lives to do your will.

Enrich us with your grace
so that, encouraging and supporting one another,
we may serve those in need
and hasten the coming of peace, love, and justice on
    earth,
through Jesus Christ our Lord.

Amen.

The Lord's Prayer may be said or sung.

Our Father in heaven,
    hallowed be your name,
    your kingdom come,
    your will be done,
        on earth as in heaven.
Give us today our daily bread.
Forgive us our sins
    as we forgive those who sin against us.
Save us from the time of trial
    and deliver us from evil.
For the kingdom, the power,
and the glory are yours,
    now and forever. Amen.

or

Our Father, who art in heaven,
    hallowed be thy name,
    thy kingdom come,
    thy will be done,
        on earth as it is in heaven.
Give us this day our daily bread;
and forgive us our debts,
    as we forgive our debtors;
and lead us not into temptation,
but deliver us from evil.
For thine is the kingdom,
    and the power, and the glory,
    forever. Amen.

Announcement of Marriage

The minister addresses the congregation:

Before God
and in the presence of this congregation,
_____ and _____ have made
    their solemn vows to each other.

They have confirmed their promises by the joining
    of hands
[and by the giving and receiving of rings].
Therefore, I proclaim that they are now husband and
    wife.

Blessed be the Father and the Son and the Holy
    Spirit now and forever.

The minister joins the couple's right hands.

The congregation may join the minister saying:

Those whom God has joined together
let no one separate.

Charge to the Couple

The minister addresses the couple:

As God's own,
clothe yourselves with compassion,
kindness, and patience,
forgiving each other
as the Lord has forgiven you,
and crown all these things with love,
which binds everything together in perfect harmony.
    (Colossians 3:12–14)

or

Whatever you do, in word or deed,
do everything in the name of the Lord Jesus,
giving thanks to God through him. (Colossians 3:17)

Benediction

The minister addresses the couple and the congregation:

The Lord bless you and keep you.
The Lord be kind and gracious to you.

The Lord look upon you with favor
and give you peace. (Numbers 6:24–26)

Amen.

or

The grace of Christ attend you,
the love of God surround you,
the Holy Spirit keep you,

that you may live in faith,
abound in hope,

and grow in love,
both now and forevermore.

Amen.

A psalm, hymn, spiritual, or anthem may be sung, or instrumental music may be played as the wedding party leaves.

Source: *Christian Marriage.* Supplemental Liturgical Resource 3. The Office of Worship for the Presbyterian Church (U.S.A.) and the Cumberland Presbyterian Church. Philadelphia: Westminster Press, 1986.

Reformed Church in America Wedding Service (1968)

ORDER OF SERVICE
FOR
THE SOLEMNIZATION OF MARRIAGE

At the proper time and place, the man and the woman to be married shall stand before the minister, the man at the right hand of the woman, when the minister shall say:

Votum

Our help is in the name of the Lord, who made heaven and earth.

Then the minister shall say to all present:

Dearly beloved, we are assembled here in the sight of God and in the presence of this company to join this man and this woman in the bonds of holy marriage; which is an honorable estate, instituted by God when he said that a man shall leave his father and his mother and shall cleave to his wife; and they shall be one flesh. It was confirmed by the words of our blessed Savior; hallowed by his presence at the marriage in Cana of Galilee; and compared by St. Paul to the mystical union between Christ and his Church. It ought not, therefore, be entered into lightly or hastily, but reverently, discreetly, and in the fear of God.

These two persons have come to be joined into this holy estate. If any man, therefore, can show just cause why they may not lawfully be joined together, let him now declare it, or else hereafter hold his peace.

Speaking to those who have come to be married, the minister shall say:

I charge you, each and both, as you shall answer to him before whom the secrets of all hearts are open, that if either of you know any reason why you may not lawfully be joined in marriage, declare it now. For be well assured that if any persons are joined together contrary to the Word of God, their marriage is not blessed of God nor is it lawful in his sight.

If no impediment appear, the minister may offer the following or some other prayer or proceed directly to the interrogation.

Prayer

Let us pray.

Almighty and eternal God, giver of all good gifts, look with favor, we pray thee, on these thy servants who lift up their hearts to thee. Enable them to make their vows to one another in all sincerity, as in thy sight, and to be faithful hereafter in keeping them, to the glory of thy holy name; through Jesus Christ our Lord. **Amen.**

Vows

The minister, before asking the questions, shall say:

Dearly Beloved, hear what the Apostle Paul says: "Wives, be subject to your husband, as to the Lord, ... as the Church is subject to Christ. ... Husbands, love your wives, as Christ loved the Church and gave himself up for her" (Ephesians 5:22, 24, 25). In the same spirit, I call on each of you to answer.

The minister, calling the man by his Christian name, shall say:

Do you, _____, take _____, before God and these witnesses, to be your wedded wife?

The man shall answer:

I do.

Will you love her, comfort her, honor and keep her, in sickness and in health, and forsaking every other, keep to her only, so long as you both shall live?

Here the man shall answer:

I will.

The minister, then, calling the woman by her Christian name, shall say:

Do you, _____, take _____, before God and these witnesses, to be your wedded husband?

The woman shall answer:

I do.

Will you love him, comfort him, honor and keep him, in sickness and in health, and forsaking every other, keep to him only, so long as you both shall live?

Here the woman shall answer:

I will.

At this point the minister may ask:

Who gives this woman to be married to this man?

The father, or guardian, of the woman may respond with "I do." The minister shall then bid the man to take the right hand of the woman and to say after him:

I, _____, take you, _____, to be my wedded wife, to have and to hold, from this day forward, for better, for worse, for richer, for poorer, in sickness and in health, to love and to cherish, till death us do part, according to God's holy ordinance; and thereto I pledge myself truly with all my heart.

Then they shall loose their hands; and the woman, with her right hand taking the man by his right hand, shall likewise say after the minister:

I, _____, take you, _____, as my wedded husband, to have and to hold, from this day forward, for better, for worse, for richer, for poorer, in sickness and in health, to love and to cherish, till death us do part, according to God's holy ordinance; and thereto I pledge myself truly with all my heart.

When a ring is used, the minister shall ask:

What token do you give of this your marriage vow?

The minister, having received the ring and given it to the man, shall bid him say:

This ring I give in token of the covenant made this day between us; in the name of the Father and of the Son and of the Holy Spirit. Amen.

or

With this ring I thee wed; in the name of the Father and of the Son and of the Holy Spirit. Amen.

If the woman also gives a ring, she shall present it in the same manner.

The minister shall now bid them join their right hands and declare:

Declaration

Forasmuch as you, _____ and _____, have covenanted together according to God's holy ordinance of marriage, and have confirmed the same by making solemn vows before God and this company and by joining hands (and by giving and receiving a ring), I pronounce you husband and wife; in the name of the Father and the Son and the Holy Spirit.

Hereafter the minister, addressing the congregation, shall say:

What therefore God has joined together, let no man put asunder. Amen.

Scripture

The minister may use the following Scripture or proceed directly to the Prayer:

Hear what the Word of God says concerning Christian love:

Love is patient and kind; love is not jealous or boastful; it is not arrogant or rude. Love does not insist on its own way; it is not irritable or resentful; it does not rejoice at wrong, but rejoices in the right. Love bears all things, believes all things, hopes all things, endures all things. (1 Corinthians 13:4–7)

Beloved, . . . love one another; for love is of God, and he who loves is born of God and knows God. He who does not love does not know God; for God is love. In this the love of God was made manifest among us, that God sent his only Son into the world, so that we might live through him. (1 John 4:7–9)

The minister, asking the man and woman to kneel, may use the following or another prayer.

Prayer

Let us pray.

O faithful God, who keepest covenant and truth with them that love thee, hear thou in heaven, thy dwelling place, the marriage vow which thy servants, _____ and _____, have vowed with thee. Grant to them the grace of thy good Spirit, that with all fidelity they may observe and keep it;

walking together in thy faith and fear, being led by the angel of thy presence and strengthened by thy hand, until they come to the inheritance of the saints in light; through Jesus Christ our Lord, who has commanded us to pray, saying:

Our Father, who art in heaven, hallowed be thy name. Thy kingdom come. Thy will be done on earth as it is in heaven. Give us this day our daily bread. And forgive us our debts, as we forgive our debtors. And lead us not into temptation, but deliver us from evil; for thine is the kingdom, and the power, and the glory, forever. Amen.

The minister shall pronounce over them one of the following benedictions.

Benediction

The peace of God that passes all understanding keep your hearts and minds in the knowledge and love of God and of his Son Jesus Christ; and the blessing of God Almighty, the Father and the Son and the Holy Spirit, be upon you and remain with you always. **Amen.**

or

The Lord bless you and keep you:
The Lord make his face to shine upon you, and be gracious to you:
The Lord lift up his countenance upon you, and give you peace.
The grace of our Lord Jesus Christ be with you. **Amen.**

or

The grace of the Lord Jesus Christ and the love of God and the fellowship of the Holy Spirit be with you. Amen.

Source: *The Liturgy of the Reformed Church in America, Together with the Psalter.* Edited by Gerrit T. Vander Lugt. Grandville, Mich.: Reformed Church Press, 1968.

Reformed Church in America Wedding Service (1987)

ORDER OF WORSHIP
FOR CHRISTIAN MARRIAGE

The Approach to God

The service of worship may begin with instrumental and/or choral music in praise of God. When the wedding party has assembled they may approach the front of the church during a

Processional Hymn

All present shall stand to sing, and remain standing through the Salutation.

Votum

Our help is in the name of the Lord who made heaven and earth. **Amen.**

Sentences

One of the following or another appropriate scriptural sentence shall be read.

I will sing of the Lord's great love forever;
with my mouth I will make your faithfulness known to all generations.
I will declare that your love stands firm forever,
that you established your faithfulness in heaven itself. (Psalm 89:1–2)

or

O servants of the Lord, you that stand in the house of the Lord, in the courts of the house of our God! Praise the Lord, for the Lord is good; sing to his name, for he is gracious! (Psalm 135:1b–3)

Salutation

Grace and peace be yours in fullest measure, through the knowledge of God and Jesus our Lord. **Amen.** (2 Peter 1:2)

Declaration of Purpose

After the people have been seated, the minister shall say:

We are gathered here to praise God for the covenant of grace and reconciliation made with us through Jesus Christ, to hear it proclaimed anew, and to respond to it as we witness the covenant of marriage _____ and _____ make with each other in Christ's name.

Christian marriage is a joyful covenanting between a man and a woman in which they proclaim, before God and human witnesses, their commitment to live together in spiritual, physical, and material unity. In this covenant they acknowledge that the great love God has shown for each of them enables them to love each other. They affirm that God's gracious presence and abiding power are needed for them to keep their vows, to continue to live in love, and to be faithful servants of Christ in this world. For human commitment is fragile and human love imperfect, but the promise of God is eternal and the love of God can bring our love to perfection.

The Word of God

Prayer

Let us pray.

Most gracious God, be with us in this time of joy and celebration. Reveal the good news of your love for us in the proclamation of your Word. Enable us to respond to you with faithfulness and obedience, so that in all we do and say your name be praised. Through Jesus Christ our Lord we pray. **Amen.**

Lessons

One or more lessons from Scripture shall be read. If there is only one lesson, it shall be from the New Testament.

Old Testament: Genesis 1:26–28, 31a; Psalm 22:25–31; Psalm 37:3–6; Isaiah 61:1–3, 10–11

Epistle: 1 Corinthians 12:31–13:8a; Ephesians 3:14–21; Colossians 3:12–17; 1 John 4:7–16

Gospel: Matthew 5:13–16; Luke 6:36–38; John 2:1–11; John 15:9–14

Sermon

The minister may preach a brief sermon relating the Word of God to the response of Christian Marriage.

Prayer for Blessing

Almighty God, through your grace write these words in our hearts, that they may bring forth in us the fruits of the Spirit, to the honor and praise of your name, through Jesus Christ our Lord. **Amen.**

The Response to God

Declaration of Consent

The persons to be married shall stand with their attendants before the minister, who shall ask the man:

_____, will you receive _____ as your wife and bind yourself to her in the covenant of marriage? Will you promise to love and honor her in true devotion; to rejoice with her in time of felicity and grieve with her in times of sorrow; and be faithful to her as long as you both shall live?

The man shall say:

I will, with the help of God.

The minister shall ask the woman:

_____, will your receive _____ as your husband and bind yourself to him in the covenant of marriage? Will you promise to love and honor him in true devotion; to rejoice with him in times of felicity and grieve with him in times of sorrow; and be faithful to him as long as you both shall live?

The woman shall say:

I will, with the help of God.

The minister shall ask the family members of the persons to be married to stand. When they have done so, the minister shall ask:

Will you receive _____ and _____ into your family and uphold them with your love as they establish themselves as a family within your own?

The family members shall say:

We will.

The minister shall ask all present to stand. When they have done so, the minister shall ask:

Will you witness this covenant between _____ and _____, respect their marriage and sustain them with your friendship and care?

All present:

We will.

Vows

The minister shall say to the man and woman:

_____ and _____, before God
and these witnesses, make your covenant of marriage with each other.

Vows may be exchanged according to Form I or Form II below.

FORM I

The man shall face the woman, take her hand in his and say:

I, _____, take you, _____, to be
   my wife,
to have and to hold from this day forward,
for better, for worse,
for richer, for poorer,
in sickness and in health,
to love and to cherish
as long as we both shall live.
To this I pledge myself
truly with all my heart.

The minister shall receive the ring from its bearer and give it to the man, who shall place it on the hand of the woman and say:

This ring I give in token of the covenant made this
day between us; in the name of the Father and of the
Son and of the Holy Spirit.

The woman, still facing the man and taking his hand in hers, shall say:

I, _____, take you, _____, to be
   my husband,
to have and to hold from this day forward,
for better, for worse,
for richer, for poorer,
in sickness and in health,
to love and to cherish
as long as we both shall live.
To this I pledge myself
truly with all my heart.

The minister shall receive the ring from its bearer and give it to the woman, who shall place it on the hand of the man and say:

This ring I give in token of the covenant made this
day between us; in the name of the Father and of the
Son and of the Holy Spirit.

or

FORM II

The man and the woman shall face each other and take hands. They shall say to each other, in turn:

_____,
I give myself to you in marriage
and vow to be your (husband/wife)
all the days of our lives.

I give you my hands
and take your hands in mine
as a symbol and pledge
of our uniting in one flesh.

I give you my love,
the outpouring of my heart,
as a symbol and pledge
of our uniting in one spirit.

I give you this ring
from out of my worldly goods
as a symbol and pledge
of our uniting as one family.

After each has said the vows, he/she shall take the ring from the minister and place it on the other's hand.

Blessing

Prayer may be offered according to Form I or Form II. The minister may ask the married persons to kneel, or to remain standing and face the minister.

FORM I

Let us ask for the blessing of the Lord.

Eternal God,
in whom we live and move and have our being;
bless _____ and _____
that they may live together in marriage
according to the vows they have made before you.

Bless them with your love,
that their love for each other
may grow ever deeper,
and their love for you may shine forth
before the world.

Bless them with your mercy,
that they may be patient and caring,
willing to share each other's joys and sorrows,
to forgive and to be forgiven,
in their life together and in the world.

Bless them with your peace,
that they may be calm and sure,
trusting in you with confident hearts
and living in harmony and concord
within their family and among all people.

Bless them with your presence,
that within their hearts and their home
Christ may reign as head,
and that they may acknowledge his Lordship
with praise and thanksgiving
now, and through all their life together,
to the glory of your holy name! **Amen.**

or

FORM II

Let us pray.

O God, Creator of life, Author of Salvation and Giver of all good gifts; look with favor upon _____ and _____ who have covenanted marriage in your name. Bless their union, and sustain them in their devotion to each other and to you.

Grant them the desire to order their lives according to your will, that in their relationship with each other, and those around them, they may show forth the joy and peace of Christ.

Sustain them in the seasons and conditions of their lives by the power of your Holy Spirit, that in joy and sorrow, leisure and labor, plenty and want, they may give thanks for your steadfast love and declare your faithfulness before the world.

Increase in them the will to grow in faith and service to Christ. Let their life together bear witness to the healing and reconciling love of Christ for this troubled, broken world.

Give them a deep appreciation of the unity of all persons within your creation, that their love for each other may be reflected also in their desire for justice, dignity and meaning for all your children.

Keep ever vivid in their hearts a vision of your kingdom, and enable them to live in the hope of its fulfillment. By the power of your Spirit, O God, accomplish these petitions as they accord with your will, for we pray through Jesus Christ our Lord. **Amen.**

Declaration

_____ and _____ have made their covenant of marriage together before God and all here present, by solemn vows, by the joining of hands, and the giving and receiving of rings. Therefore, I declare that they are husband and wife; in the name of the Father and of the Son and of the Holy Spirit.

and (to the couple)

Be united; live in peace, and the God of peace and love will be with you. (2 Corinthians 12:11)

or (to all present)

They are no longer two, therefore, but one body. So then, what God has united, no one may divide. **Amen.** (Matthew 19:6)

Peace

The husband and wife greet each other with the kiss of peace.

Benediction

The grace of the Lord Jesus Christ, the love of God, and the fellowship of the Holy Spirit be with you all. **Amen.** (2 Corinthians 12:13)

Recessional Hymn

A hymn of thanksgiving may be sung, or instrumental music played, during which the married persons and their attendants may recess.

Source: *Worship the Lord*. The Reformed Church in America. Grandville, Mich.: Reformed Church Press, 1987.

United Church of Canada Wedding Service (1950)

AN ORDER FOR
THE SOLEMNIZATION OF MATRIMONY

At the time appointed for the Solemnization of Matrimony, the persons to be married, standing together, the man on the right and the woman on the left, the Minister shall say,

The Introduction

Dearly beloved, we are gathered here in the presence of God to join together this man and this woman in Holy Matrimony; which is an honorable estate, ordained of God unto the fulfilling and perfecting of the love of man and woman in mutual honor and forbearance; and therefore it is not by any to be taken in hand lightly, or thoughtlessly, but reverently, discreetly, soberly, and in the fear of God.

Into which holy estate these two persons present come now to be joined.

Therefore if any man can show just cause, why they may not lawfully be joined together, let him now speak, or else hereafter for ever hold his peace.

Then speaking to the persons that are to be married the Minister shall say,

I require and charge you both, before the great God the Searcher of all hearts, that if either of you know any impediment, why ye may not lawfully be joined together in Marriage, ye do now confess it. For be ye well assured that so many as are joined together otherwise than as God's Word doth allow, are not joined together by God; neither is their union blessed by him.

The Marriage

If no impediment be alleged, then shall the Minister say unto the man,

_____, wilt thou have this woman to be thy wedded wife, to live together after God's ordinance in the holy estate of Matrimony? Wilt thou love her, comfort her, honor and keep her, in sickness and in health? and, forsaking all other, keep thee only unto her, so long as ye both shall live?

The man shall answer,

I will.

Then shall the Minister say unto the woman,

_____, wilt thou have this man to be thy wedded husband, to live together after God's ordinance in the holy estate of Matrimony? Wilt thou love him, comfort him, honor and keep him, in sickness and in health? and, forsaking all other, keep thee only unto him, so long as ye both shall live?

The woman shall answer,

I will.

142

Then shall the Minister say,

Who giveth this woman to be married to this man?

Then shall they plight their troth to each other in this manner.

The Minister shall cause the man with his right hand to take the woman by her right hand and to say after him as followeth.

I, _____, take thee, _____, to be my wedded wife, to have and to hold from this day forward, for better, for worse; for richer, for poorer; in sickness and in health; to love and to cherish, till death us do part, according to God's holy ordinance; and thereto I plight thee my troth.

Then shall they loose their hands; and the woman with her right hand taking the man by his right hand shall likewise say after the Minister,

I, _____, take thee, _____, to be my wedded husband, to have and to hold from this day forward, for better, for worse; for richer, for poorer; in sickness and in health; to love and to cherish, till death us do part, according to God's holy ordinance; and thereto I plight thee my troth.

Then they shall again loose their hands; and the man shall give to the woman a ring, putting it upon the fourth finger of her left hand; and holding it there, shall say after the Minister,

This ring I give thee in token of the covenant made this day between us: In the name of the Father, and of the Son, and of the Holy Spirit. Amen.

Then may the man and the woman kneel down; but the People shall remain standing. And the minister shall say,

Let us pray.

O Eternal God, Creator and Preserver of all mankind, giver of all spiritual grace, the author of everlasting life; Send thy blessing upon these thy servants, this man and this woman, whom we bless in thy name; that, living faithfully together, they may surely perform and keep the vow and covenant betwixt them made; and may ever remain in perfect love and peace together, and live according to thy law; through Jesus Christ our Lord. **Amen.**

Then shall the Minister join their right hands together, and say,

Those whom God hath joined together let not man put asunder.

Then shall the Minister speak unto the People.

Forasmuch as _____, and _____, have consented together in holy wedlock, and have witnessed the same before God and this company, and thereto have given and pledged their troth either to other, and have declared the same by giving and receiving of a ring, and by joining of hands; I pronounce that they be man and wife together, In the name of the Father, and of the Son, and of the Holy Ghost. Amen.

And the Minister shall add this Blessing.

God the Father, Son, and Holy Spirit, bless, preserve, and keep you; the Lord mercifully with his favor look upon you; and so fill you with all spiritual benediction and grace, that ye may so live together in this life, that in the world to come ye may have life everlasting. **Amen.**

Or this.

The Lord bless you, and keep you: the Lord make his face to shine upon you, and be gracious unto you: the Lord lift up his countenance upon you, and give you peace. **Amen.**

Source: *The Book of Common Order of the United Church of Canada.* Toronto: United Church Publishing House, 1950.

United Church of Canada Wedding Service (1985 Rite I)

MARRIAGE SERVICE

The people will join in those parts of the service printed in bold type.

Gathering

Prelude

Processional Hymn

> *The wedding party may enter during the hymn. The people stand.*

Greeting

> *All remain standing. The presider greets the community with scripture sentences appropriate to the occasion and/or the following dialogue:*

The grace of our Lord Jesus Christ, and the love of God, and the communion of the Holy Spirit, be with you all.

And also with you.

Purpose

> *The people are seated. The persons to be married shall stand before the presider.*

Friends, we are gathered here in the presence of God to witness the marriage of _____ and _____ and to ask God's blessing upon them.

Marriage is a gift of God and a means of God's grace, in which man and woman become one flesh. It is God's purpose that, as husband and wife give themselves to each other in love, they shall grow together and be united in that love, as Christ is united with his Church.

The union of man and woman in heart, body, and mind is intended for their mutual comfort and help, that they may know each other with delight and tenderness in acts of love (and that they may be blessed in the procreation, care, and upbringing of children).

In marriage, husband and wife give themselves to each other, to care for each other in good times and in bad. They are linked to each other's families, and they begin a new life together in the community. It is a way of life that all should reverence, and none should lightly undertake.

We acknowledge that because of human frailty and sin, the gladness of marriage can be overcast. Yet the God who brings light out of darkness can turn our grief into joy.

We rejoice that marriage is given by God, blessed by our Lord Jesus Christ, and sustained by the Holy Spirit.

> *A rite of confession may be used as indicated in the Guidelines.*

Declaration of Intent

The presider shall say to the persons who are to marry:

_____ and _____, you have made it known that you wish to be joined together in marriage. If either of you, or anyone here present, can show just cause why you may not lawfully be married, now is the time to declare it.

The presider shall say to the woman:

_____, will you have this man to be your husband?

The woman answers:

I will.

The presider shall say to the man:

_____, will you have this woman to be your wife?

The man answers:

I will.

The parents, or those chosen to represent the immediate family, are invited to stand and the presider shall say:

Do you, the families of these two persons, give them your blessing and promise to uphold and care for them in their marriage?

The parents answer:

We do.

The people are invited to stand and the presider shall say:

Do you, the friends of these two persons, give them your blessing and promise to support and honor them in their marriage?

The people answer:

We do.

Prayer

A collect for the day or season may be used, or the prayer that follows:

God our Creator, you have made us in your own image, with a mind to understand your works, a heart to love you, and a will to serve you: increase in us that knowledge, that love, and that obedience, that we may grow daily in your likeness; through Jesus Christ our Savior.

Amen.

Service of the Word

The persons to be married and their attendants may be seated.

Scripture Lessons

Passages from the Scriptures may be read, including at least one from each of the Old and New Testaments.

Music

A hymn, psalm, canticle, anthem, or other music may be sung or played before or after the readings.

Sermon or Homily

Marriage

Prayer

The persons to be married shall stand before the presider and the presider may say:

Almighty God, you send your Holy Spirit to fill the life of all your people. Open the hearts of these your children to the riches of your grace, that they may bring forth the fruit of the Spirit in love, joy, and peace through Jesus Christ our Lord.

Amen.

Vows

The man and woman shall face each other, joining their right hands, and each shall say after the presider:

In the presence of God and before these witnesses, I, _____, take you, _____, to be my husband/wife, to have and to hold from this day forward, for better, for worse; for richer, for poorer;

in sickness and in health; in joy and in sorrow; to love and to cherish, as long as we both shall live. This is my solemn vow

Rings

The presider shall say:

Bless, O God, the giving of these rings, that those who wear them may live in faithfulness and love all their days, through Jesus Christ our Savior.

Amen.

Each partner shall give a ring to the other, placing it on the fourth finger of the left hand and saying:

I give you this ring as a sign of our covenant. With all that I am, and all that I have, I honor you.

Kiss

The man and woman may kiss each other as a sign of their marriage.

Declaration

The presider shall say:

_____ and _____ have made a covenant of marriage before God and in the presence of all of us. They have confirmed their marriage by the joining of hands, by the exchange of rings, and by the giving of a kiss. Therefore, I declare them to be husband and wife.

Blessing

May God bless, preserve, and keep you; may God look upon you with favor; may God fill you with all blessings and give you grace that you may in this life live together in joy, and in the world to come have life everlasting.

Amen.

Signing of Documents

The documents may be signed in the presence of the congregation.

Signs of Affirmation

The presider may say:

Greet _____ and _____ who are now joined in marriage.

The people may respond with applause.

A hymn may be sung.

Prayers of the People

This prayer may he led by someone other than the presider.

Let us pray.

Almighty God, in whom we live and move and have our being: look graciously upon the world which you have made, and for which your Son gave his life; and especially on all whom you make to be one flesh in holy marriage. May their lives together be a sacrament of your love in this broken world, a sign of unity overcoming estrangement, forgiveness healing guilt, and joy vanquishing despair.
God, in your mercy,
Hear our prayer.

May _____ and _____ so live together, that the strength of their love may enrich our common life and become a sign of your faithfulness.
God, in your mercy,
Hear our prayer.

(May they receive the gift and heritage of children and the grace to bring them up to know and love you.)
God, in your mercy,
Hear our prayer.

May their home be a place of truth, security, and love; and their lives an example of concern for others.
God, in your mercy,
Hear our prayer.

May those who have witnessed these vows find their lives strengthened and their loyalties confirmed.
God, in your mercy,
Hear our prayer.

Additional prayers may be offered:

The leader may conclude the prayer with words such as these:

Gracious and loving God, with Christ your Son you have made us your sons and daughters. Help us to build the world entrusted to our care into the one family of Jesus Christ. We ask this in Christ's name. **Amen.**

or

Loving God, there is no joy that does not come from your hand, no pain that does not echo in your heart. See our needs and give us strength to work with you and with each other in building a world where love can live. We ask this through Christ our Savior. **Amen.**

The Service continues with one of the following options:

A. Thanksgiving

The presider may say:

Friends, let us give thanks to our God.
Thanks be to God.

Here may the following or other prayers be said:

Most gracious God,
we give you thanks for your tender love
in sending Jesus Christ to come among us,
to be born of human mother,
and to make the way of the cross to be the way of
  life.
We thank you, also, for consecrating
the union of man and woman in his Name.
By the power of your Holy Spirit,
pour out the abundance of your blessing
upon this man and woman.
Defend them from every enemy.
Lead them into all peace.
Let their love for each other be
a seal upon their hearts,
a mantle about their shoulders,
and a crown upon their foreheads.
Bless them in their work and in their companionship;
in their sleeping and in their waking;

in their joys and in their sorrows;
in their life and in their death.
Finally, in your mercy, bring them to that table
where your saints feast for ever
in your heavenly home;
through Jesus Christ our Lord,
who with you and the Holy Spirit lives and reigns,
one God, for ever and ever.
Amen.

The Lord's Prayer

Blessing and Sending Forth

The presider may say:

The grace of Christ attend you;
the love of God surround you;
the Holy Spirit keep you.

The presider or another leader may dismiss the people saying:

Go forth in the name of Christ.
Thanks be to God.

or

Go in peace to love and serve the Lord.
Thanks be to God.

A hymn may be sung or instrumental music played as the people leave.

B. Service of the Table

The Peace

The presider may address the people with these or other words:

Let us stand and greet one another with signs of love and reconciliation.

or a dialogue may be used such as:

The peace of the Lord be with you always.
And also with you.

All stand and exchange signs and words of God's peace with an embrace or clasp of the hands and the words:

The peace of Christ *or* **Peace.**

Presenting of the Gifts

The presider may say:

As forgiven and reconciled people let us with joy present our gifts of bread and wine at the Lord's Table.

A hymn or instrumental music, dance, or other acts may accompany the presentation of the gifts which are brought forward to the table by the wife and husband or other members of the community.

The Great Thanksgiving

The Lord be with you.
And also with you.
Lift up your hearts.
We lift them to the Lord.
Let us give thanks to the Lord our God.
It is right to give God thanks and praise.

We thank you God,
Father and Mother of us all.
From the beginning you made the world and all its
    creatures;
You made people to live for you and for one another.
You gave Adam and Eve to each other
that they need not be alone.
With Abraham and Sarah you made a covenant
that through them all people might be blessed.
To Mary and Joseph you gave a Son
who has wedded all people to yourself.
Therefore, with your people in all ages
and the whole company of heaven,
we join in the song of unending praise:

Holy, holy, holy Lord, God of power and might,
heaven and earth are full of your glory.
Hosanna in the highest.
Blessed is the one who comes in the name of the
    Lord.
Hosanna in the highest.

Blessed are you, gracious God,
because you loved the world so much
you gave yourself in Jesus Christ,
who gave all that he was
that we might be one with you.

He won for you a new people to be his family,
and in his sacrifice showed us the height and
depth and breadth of covenant love.
He suffered and died for the sin of the world.
You raised him from the dead
that we, too, might have new life.
He ascended to be with you in glory
and, by the power of your Holy Spirit,
is with us always.

On the night he offered himself up for us,
he took bread, gave thanks to you, broke it,
gave it to his disciples, and said:
"Take, eat; this is my body which is given for you.
Do this in remembrance of me."
When supper was over,
he took the cup, gave thanks to you,
gave it to his disciples, and said:
"Drink from this, all of you;
this cup is the new covenant sealed by my blood,
poured out for you and many,
for the forgiveness of sins.
Whenever you drink it,
do this in remembrance of me."
Therefore,
in remembrance of all your mighty acts in Jesus
    Christ,
we ask you to accept
this sacrifice of praise and thanksgiving,
which we offer in union with Christ's sacrifice for us,
as a living and holy surrender of ourselves.

Send the power of your Holy Spirit on us
and on these gifts.
May the sharing of this bread and wine
be for us a sharing in the body and blood of Christ.
Pour out your blessing upon _____ and

_____.

May they sing a new song of your great love in
    communion with you
and all your saints in heaven and earth.
May their love for each other proclaim love of Christ.
May the faithful service of all your people bring
    justice, joy, and love to all the world.
Gather us into the one great family whom Christ is
    calling to the heavenly marriage feast prepared for
    all the faithful.

Through Christ, with Christ, and in Christ, in the unity of the Holy Spirit, all glory is yours, God most holy, now and forever. **Amen.**

The Lord's Prayer

The traditional form may be used or the new ecumenical version:

Our Father in heaven,
 hallowed be your Name,
 your kingdom come,
 your will be done,
 on earth as in heaven.
Give us today our daily bread.
Forgive us our sins
 as we forgive those
 who sin against us.
Save us from the time of trial,
 and deliver us from evil.
For the kingdom, the power,
 and the glory are yours,
 now and for ever. Amen.

Breaking of the Bread and Pouring the Wine

The presider takes the bread and breaks it in silence or with the following words:

The body of Christ broken for you

or

The bread which we break is the communion of the body of Christ.

The presider takes the cup and pours the wine in silence or with the following words:

The blood of Christ poured out for you

or

The cup of blessing which we bless is the communion of the blood of Christ.

Members of the community may assist in breaking the bread and preparing the cups for distribution. When everything is ready the presider may invite the people to communion with the words:

The Gifts of God for the people of God

and/or

Come, for all things are now ready.

Sharing of the Bread and the Cup

The bread and wine are served with the following words:

The body of Christ, (given for you)
The blood of Christ, (shed for you)

or

The body of Christ, the bread of heaven
The blood of Christ, the cup of salvation

*The communicant responds each time, **Amen**, and then receives.*

Prayer after Communion

All may stand and say together:

Loving God,
we thank you that you have fed us in this sacrament,
united us with Christ, and given us a foretaste of the marriage feast of the Lamb.
Send us out in the power of your Spirit to live and work to your praise and glory.
Amen.

Sending Forth

Blessing

The presider may say:

May the blessing of the God of Abraham and Sarah and of the Son, born of our sister, Mary, and of the Holy Spirit who broods over the world as a mother over her children, be upon you and remain with you always.
Amen.

Sending Forth

Go in peace to love and serve the Lord.
Amen.

A hymn may be sung or instrumental music may be played as the people leave.

"The Celebration of Marriage" (pamphlet). The United Church of Canada. The Working Unit on Worship and Liturgy, Division of Mission in Canada. 1985.

United Church of Canada Wedding Service (1985 Rite II)

MARRIAGE SERVICE

The people will join in those parts of the service printed in bold type.

Prelude

Entrance

The entrance of the wedding party may be accompanied by instrumental music or singing. The persons to be married shall stand before the presider.

Greeting

The presider may say:

May God who gives life to all creation and who hears all prayers be with us.

Purpose

The people may be seated.

Friends, we are gathered here in the presence of God to witness the marriage of _____ and _____ and to ask God to bless them.

The bond of marriage was given by God who created us to be in covenant. We acknowledge the reality of human failure; yet we affirm the joy and freedom of lifelong union. In the assurance of God's promise to be with us, let us open our hearts in faithfulness and in hope.

Declaration of Intent

The presider shall say to the persons who are to marry:

_____ and _____, you have made it known that you wish to be joined together in marriage. If either of you, or anyone here present, can show just cause why you may not lawfully be married, now is the time to declare it.

The presider shall say to the woman:

_____, will you have this man to be your husband?

The woman answers:

I will.

The presider shall say to the man:

_____, will you have this woman to be your wife?

The man answers:

I will.

The parents, or those chosen to represent the immediate family, are invited to stand and the presider shall say:

Do you, the families of these two persons, give them your blessing, and promise to uphold and care for them in their marriage?

The parents answer:

We do.

The people are invited to stand and the presider shall say:

Do you, the friends of these two persons, give them your blessing and promise to support and honor them in their marriage?

The people answer:

We do.

Prayer

A collect for the day or season may be used, or the prayer that follows:

Creator of all, you have made us in your image, and
    have made the world as our home.
You give us love and courage, joy and faithfulness,
    hope and comfort.
We give you thanks for these gifts and we praise you
    for your goodness.
Be with us, that we may become ever more fully the
    people you have created us to be.
This we pray through Jesus Christ our Lord.
Amen.

Readings

The persons to be married may be seated. At least one reading shall be from scripture.

Music

A hymn, psalm, anthem, or other music may be sung or played before or after the readings.

Address

The nature of marriage generally and this marriage in particular may be expressed in a variety of ways such as word, music, and/or dance.

Prayer

The persons to be married shall stand before the presider and the presider shall say:

Loving and beloved God, from the beginning you have made us to live in partnership with one another. We pray for the presence of your Spirit with these two persons. Fill their hearts with sincerity and truth as they enter this solemn covenant.
Amen.

Vows

The man and woman shall face each other and join their right hands, and each shall say after the presider:

_____, I commit myself to be with you in joy and adversity, in wholeness and brokenness, in peace and trouble, living with you in fidelity and love all our days.

Rings

Each partner shall give a ring to the other, placing it on the fourth finger of the left hand and saying:

I give you this ring that you may wear it as a symbol of the vows we have made this day.

Kiss

The man and woman may kiss each other as a sign of their marriage.

Declaration

The presider may say:

_____ and _____ have made a covenant of marriage before God and in the presence of all of us. They have confirmed their marriage by the joining of hands, by the exchange of rings, and by the giving of a kiss. Therefore, I declare them to be husband and wife.

Blessing

May there be truth and understanding between you. May you enjoy length of days, fulfilment of hopes, and peace and contentment of mind. May God bless and keep you always.

Signing of the Documents

The documents may be signed in the presence of the assembly.

Signs of Affirmation

The presider may say:

Greet _____ and _____ who are
now joined in marriage.

The people may respond with applause.

Prayers

*This prayer or another may be led by someone other than
the presider.*

Spirit of God, in whom we live and move and have
 our being,
you have given us life and the grace of human love
 that draws us to each other.

Today we pray for _____ and
_____ in their life together.
We are thankful for the joy they find in each other
and for the hope they declare in this act of marriage.

May they always be strengthened
to keep the vows they have made,
to cherish the life they share, and
to honor each other in love.
Amen.

The Lord's Prayer

Dismissal

The grace of Christ attend you;
the love of God surround you;
the Holy Spirit keep you.
Amen.

*A hymn may be sung or instrumental music may be
played as the people leave.*

"The Celebration of Marriage" (pamphlet). The United Church of
Canada. The Working Unit on Worship and Liturgy, Division of
Mission in Canada. 1985.

United Church of Christ Wedding Service (1969)

THE ORDER FOR MARRIAGE

A processional hymn may be sung as the persons to be married present themselves before the minister, the man standing at the right hand of the woman.

The minister shall say:

In the name of the Father, and of the Son, and of the Holy Spirit. **Amen.**

or

Our help is in the name of the Lord who made heaven and earth. **Amen.**

Dearly beloved, we are gathered together in the sight of God to join this man and this woman in marriage. Let all who enter it know that marriage is a sacred and joyous covenant, a way of life ordained of God from the beginning of his creation. "For this reason," says the Lord, "a man shall leave his father and mother and be joined to his wife, and the two shall become one flesh. What therefore God has joined together, let no man put asunder." Marriage is also compared by the apostle Paul to the mystical union between Christ and his church. Therefore, it should not be entered into unadvisedly or lightly, but reverently, considering the purposes for which it was ordained.

God has ordered the covenant of marriage: that husband and wife may give to each other companionship, help, and comfort, both in prosperity and in adversity; that he may hallow the expression of the natural affections; that children may be born and nurtured in families and trained in godliness; and that human society may stand on firm foundations.

Into this sacred covenant these two persons now desire to enter. Let us therefore invoke the blessing of God on the union now to be formed.

The minister shall offer the following or another prayer:

Let us pray.

Almighty and most merciful Father, we your unworthy children praise you for all the bounties of your providence, and for all the gifts of your grace. We thank you especially for the institution of marriage, which you have ordained to guard, to hallow, and to perfect the gift of love. We thank you for the joy which these your servants find in each other, and for the love and trust in which they enter this holy covenant. And since without your help we cannot do anything as we ought, we pray you to enrich your servants with your grace, that they may enter into their marriage as in your sight, and truly keep their vows; through Jesus Christ our Lord. **Amen.**

The minister shall say to the man:

_____, will you have this woman to be your wife, and be faithful to her alone?

The man shall answer:

I will, with the help of God.

The minister shall say to the woman:

153

_____, will you have this man to be your husband, and be faithful to him alone?

The woman shall answer:

I will, with the help of God.

If the woman is given in marriage by her parent or guardian, the minister shall say:

Who gives this woman to be married to this man?

The person who gives the woman shall answer:

I do.

A hymn may be sung.

The following lesson, or another from holy scripture, shall be read, the minister saying:

Hear the word of God in the fifth chapter of the letter to the Ephesians, beginning at the twenty-first verse:

Be subject to one another out of reverence for Christ. Wives, be subject to your husbands, as to the Lord. For the husband is the head of the wife as Christ is the head of the church, his body, and is himself its Savior. As the church is subject to Christ, so let wives also be subject in everything to their husbands. Husbands, love your wives, as Christ loved the church and gave himself up for her, that he might sanctify her, having cleansed her by the washing of water with the word, that the church might be presented before him in splendor, without spot or wrinkle or any such thing, that she might be holy and without blemish. Even so husbands should love their wives as their own bodies. He who loves his wife loves himself. For no man ever hates his own flesh, but nourishes and cherishes it, as Christ does the church, because we are members of his body. "For this reason a man shall leave his father and mother and be joined to his wife, and the two shall become one." This is a great mystery, and I take it to mean Christ and the church; however, let each one of you love his wife as himself, and let the wife see that she respects her husband.

Alternate or additional passages suggested as appropriate are: Romans 12:1–3, 9–13; 1 Corinthians 13:4–8a; 1 John 4:7–12; Matthew 5:2–9.

A sermon may be preached.

The Statement of Faith or the Apostles' Creed may be said.

The two shall make their covenant in this manner: they shall join right hands, and the man shall say:

I, _____, take you, _____, to be my wife, and I promise to love and sustain you in the bonds of marriage from this day forward, in sickness and in health, in plenty and in want, in joy and in sorrow, till death shall part us, according to God's holy ordinance.

The woman shall say:

I, _____, take you, _____, to be my husband, and I promise to love and sustain you in the bonds of marriage from this day forward, in sickness and in health, in plenty and in want, in joy and in sorrow, till death shall part us, according to God's holy ordinance.

The minister shall now receive the ring and give it to the man to place on the woman's left hand.

The man shall say:

This ring I give you in token of my faithfulness and love, and as a pledge to honor you with my whole being, and to share with you my worldly goods.

or

I give you this ring in token of the covenant made today between us; in the name of the Father, and of the Son, and of the Holy Spirit.

If two rings are to be used, the minister shall now receive the second ring and give it to the woman to place on the man's left hand.

The woman shall say:

This ring I give you [*when only one ring is used, the word "receive" shall be substituted for the words "give you"*] in token of my faithfulness and love, and as a pledge to honor you with my whole being, and to share with you my worldly goods.

or

I give you (I receive) this ring in token of the covenant made today between us; in the name of the Father, and of the Son, and of the Holy Spirit.

The minister shall lay his right hand on their joined right hands and say:

Forasmuch as you, _____ and _____, have consented together in this sacred covenant, and have declared the same before God and this company, I pronounce you husband and wife, in the name of the Father, and of the Son, and of the Holy Spirit. **Amen.**

The man and the woman may kneel.

The minister shall say:

God the Father, God the Son, and God the Holy Spirit bless, preserve, and keep you; the Lord mercifully with his favor look upon you, and fill you with all spiritual benediction and grace, that you may so live together in this life, that in the world to come you may have life everlasting. **Amen.**

Let us pray.

Almighty and most merciful God, having now united this man and woman in the holy covenant of marriage, grant them grace to live therein according to your holy word; strengthen them in constant faithfulness and true affection toward each other; sustain and defend them in all trials and temptations; and help them so to pass through this world in faith toward you, in communion with your church, and in loving service one of the other, that they may enjoy forever your heavenly benediction; through Jesus Christ our Lord. **Amen.**

Our Father, who art in heaven, hallowed be thy name. Thy kingdom come. Thy will be done on earth as it is in heaven. Give us this day our daily bread. And forgive us our debts, as we forgive our debtors. And lead us not into temptation, but deliver us from evil. For thine is the kingdom, and the power, and the glory, forever. **Amen.**

The minister shall say:

The peace of God, which passes all understanding, keep your hearts and minds in the knowledge and love of God, and of his Son Jesus Christ our Lord; and the blessing of God Almighty, the Father, the Son, and the Holy Spirit, be with you, and remain with you always. **Amen.**

It shall be the duty of the minister to confer beforehand with the persons to be married, counseling them in the meaning of Christian marriage.

The laws respecting marriage being different in the several states, the minister is referred to the direction of those laws in fulfilling the accompanying civil contract between the persons.

Source: *Services of the Church*. Published by the Division of Publication, United Church Board for Homeland Ministries for the Executive Council and the Commission on Worship, United Church of Christ. New York: United Church Press, 1969.

United Church of Christ Wedding Service (1986)

ORDER FOR MARRIAGE

Prelude

Entrance

Banners, ribbons, flowers, candles, white carpeting, or other items may be used in the procession in accordance with local custom. A hymn, psalm, canticle, or anthem may be sung, or instrumental music may be played.

The couple to be married may enter the sanctuary together or separately. They may be accompanied by their parents, other members of the family, and friends. People in the congregation who are able may stand for the processional.

Greeting

The couple to be married and the wedding party may stand, if they are able, facing the one presiding. Usually the groom is at the right of the bride as they face forward.

The one presiding may use one of the following greetings or another one based on scripture.

(A)

Pastor

The grace of our Lord Jesus Christ and the love of God and the communion of the Holy Spirit be with you all.

People

And also with you.

(B)

Pastor

Love comes from God. Everyone who truly loves is a child of God. Let us worship God.

Introduction

The one presiding may state the Christian understanding of marriage, using one of the following or other words.

(A)

Pastor

Dearly beloved, we are gathered here as the people of God to witness the marriage of _____ and _____.

We come to share in their joy and to ask God to bless them.

Marriage is a gift of God, sealed by a sacred covenant. God gives human love. Through that love, husband and wife come to know each other with mutual care and companionship. God gives joy. Through that joy, wife and husband may share their new life with others as Jesus shared new wine at the wedding in Cana.

With our love and our prayers, we support _____ and _____ as they now freely give themselves to each other.

(B)

Pastor

Dear friends, we have come together in the presence of God to witness the marriage of _____ and _____, to surround them with our prayers, and to share in their joy.

The scriptures teach us that the bond and covenant of marriage is a gift of God, a holy mystery in which man and woman become one flesh, an image of the union of Christ and the church.

As this woman and this man give themselves to each other today, we remember that at Cana in Galilee our Savior Jesus Christ made the wedding feast a sign of God's reign of love.

Let us enter into this celebration confident that through the Holy Spirit, Christ is present with us now. We pray that this couple may fulfill God's purpose for the whole of their lives.

Prayer

One of these, a prayer of confession with an assurance of pardon, or a prayer for illumination may be offered.

Pastor

Let us pray.

(A)

All

O God, we gather to celebrate your gift of love and its presence among us. We rejoice that two people have chosen to commit themselves to a life of loving faithfulness to one another. We praise you, O God, for the ways you have touched our lives with a variety of loving relationships. We give thanks that we have experienced your love through the life-giving love

of Jesus Christ and through the care and affection of other people.

At the same time, we remember and confess to you, O God, that we often have failed to be loving, that we often have taken for granted the people for whom we care most. We selfishly neglect and strain the bonds that unite us with others.

We hurt those who love us and withdraw from the community that encircles us. Forgive us, O God. Renew within us an affectionate spirit. Enrich our lives with the gracious gift of your love so that we may embrace others with the same love. May our participation in this celebration of love and commitment give to us a new joy and responsiveness to the relationships we cherish; through Jesus Christ we pray. Amen.

Pastor

Through the great depth and strength of God's love for us, God reaches out to us to forgive our sins and to restore us to life. Be assured, children of God, that God's love enfolds us and upbuilds us so that we may continue to love one another as God has loved us.

(B)

All

Gracious God, always faithful in your love for us, we rejoice in your presence. You create love. You unite us in one human family. You offer your word and lead us in light. You open your loving arms and embrace us with strength. May the presence of Christ fill our hearts with new joy and make new the lives of your servants whose marriage we celebrate. Bless all creation through this sign of your love shown in the love of _____ and _____ for each other. May the power of your Holy Spirit sustain them and all of us in love that knows no end. Amen.

Reading of Scripture

The congregation may be seated. One or more scripture lessons may be read by the one presiding, by members of the family, or by members of the wedding party. If Holy

Communion is to be celebrated, it is appropriate that the readings include a Gospel lesson. A hymn, psalm, or other music may be offered between readings or before or after the sermon. Passages for consideration for use include the following ecumenical suggestions.

Old Testament

Genesis 1:26–28, 31; 2:18–24
Psalms 23; 33; 34; 37:3–7; 67; 100; 103; 112; 117;
   121; 127; 128; 136; 145; 148; 150
Song of Solomon 2:8–13; 8:6–7
Jeremiah 31:31–34
Isaiah 54:5–8
Hosea 2:16–23

Epistles

Romans 8:31–39; 12:1–2, 9–18
1 Corinthians 6:15–20; 13:1–13
Ephesians 3:14–21; 5:2, 21–33
Colossians 3:12–17
1 Peter 3:1–9
1 John 3:18–24; 4:7–16
Revelation 19:1, 5–9

Gospels

Matthew 5:1–12; 5:13–16; 7:21, 24–29; 19:3–6; 22:
   35–40
Mark 10:6–9, 13–16
John 2:1–11; 15:9–17

Sermon

A brief sermon, charge, or other response to scripture may be given.

Depending on the religious affiliations of those gathered for the marriage service, it may be appropriate for all who are able to stand and say a creed or affirmation of faith. Forms of the United Church of Christ Statement of Faith, historic creeds, and other affirmations can be found in the Book of Worship of the United Church of Christ.

Declaration of Intention

Pastor, addressing the couple

Before God and this congregation,
I ask you to affirm your willingness
to enter this covenant of marriage
and to share all the joys and sorrows
of this new relationship,
whatever the future may hold.

Pastor, addressing the groom

_____,

will you have _____ to be your wife,
and will you love her faithfully
as long as you both shall live?

Groom

I will, with the help of God.

Pastor, addressing the bride

_____,

will you have _____ to be your husband,
and will you love him faithfully,
as long as you both shall live?

Bride

I will, with the help of God.

Pledge of Support

This pledge of support should be used at the discretion of the pastor and in consultation with the people involved. It allows the family and congregation to pledge their support and encouragement to the couple. It is important to consider use of the pledge when there are children from previous relationships.

•

Children who will share in the new family may be addressed in these or similar words. They may stand, if able, at their places or may move near the couple.

Pastor, addressing each child by name

_____,

you are entering a new family.
Will you give to this new family
your trust, love, and affection?

Each child

I will, with the help of God.

Pastor, addressing the bride and groom

_____ and _____,
will you be faithful and loving parents
to _____?

Couple

We will, with the help of God.

•

The pastor may invite the immediate families of the groom and bride, including adults or younger children from previous relationships, to stand in place, if they are able, and to offer their support in these or similar words.

Pastor, addressing the families

Will the families of _____ and

_____

(please stand/please answer) in support of this
   couple.
Do you offer your prayerful blessing
and loving support to this marriage?
If so, please say, "I do."

Family members

I do.

All family members may be seated. The person(s) who escorted the bride may be seated with her family.

The pastor may address the congregation in these or similar words.

Pastor, addressing the congregation

Do you, as people of God,
pledge your support and encouragement
to the covenant commitment that
_____ and _____ are making
   together?
If so, please say, "We do."

People

We do.

An intercessory prayer, using the following or other words, may be offered.

Pastor

God of our mothers and of our fathers,
hear our pledges encouraging and supporting this
   union
of _____ and _____.

Bless us as we offer our prayerful
and loving support to their marriage.
Bless them as they pledge their lives to each other.
With faith in you and in each other,
may this couple always bear witness
to the reality of the love
to which we witness this day.
May their love continue to grow,
and may it be a true reflection
of your love for us all;
through Jesus Christ.
Amen.

Vows of the Marriage Covenant

The pastor may introduce the covenant promises in the following or similar words.

(A)

Pastor

_____ and _____, by your cov-
enant promises shared with us, unite yourselves
in marriage and be subject to one another out of
reverence for Christ.

(B)

Pastor

_____ and _____, speak your
covenant promises that you have come to offer before God.

If able, the couple may face each other and join hands, the women first giving her bouquet, if any, to an attendant. The groom and bride may say these or other words of covenant.

Bride

_____,
I give myself to you

to be your wife.
I promise to love and sustain you
in the covenant of marriage,
from this day forward,
in sickness and in health,
in plenty and in want,
in joy and in sorrow,
as long as we both shall live.

> *Groom*

_____,
I give myself to you
to be your husband.
I promise to love and sustain you
in the covenant of marriage,
from this day forward,
in sickness and in health,
in plenty and in want,
in joy and in sorrow,
as long as we both shall live.

Exchange of Symbols

> *It is recommended that the giving and receiving of rings or other symbols be shared equally by both bride and groom.*

> *Pastor*

_____ and _____,
what will you share to symbolize your love?

> *The groom and bride may name the symbol(s) and present them/it to the pastor, who may hold or place a hand on the symbol(s) and offer one of these or another prayer.*

(A)

> *Pastor*

By (these symbols/this symbol) of covenant promise, Gracious God, remind _____ and _____ of your encircling love and unending faithfulness that in all their life together they may know joy and peace in one another.

> *People*

Amen.

(B)

> *Pastor*

Eternal God, who in the time of Noah gave us the rainbow as a sign of promise, bless (these symbols/this symbol) that (they/it) also may be (signs/a sign) of promises fulfilled in lives of faithful loving; through Jesus Christ our Savior.

> *People*

Amen.

> *If both husband and wife receive symbols, options A and B are used.*

(A)

> *Groom*

_____,
I give you (this/these) _____
as a sign of my love and faithfulness.

> *Bride*

I receive (this/these) _____
as a sign of our love and faithfulness.

(B)

> *Bride*

_____,
I give you (this/these) _____
as a sign of my love and faithfulness.

> *Groom*

I receive (this/these) _____
as a sign of our love and faithfulness.

Announcement of Marriage

> *If able, the couple may stand or kneel and join hands, and the pastor may place a hand on their joined hands while announcing the marriage, using one of these or other words.*

(A)

Pastor, addressing the couple

_____ and _____, you have committed yourselves to each other in this joyous and sacred covenant. Become one. Fulfill your promises. Love and serve God, honor Christ and each other, and rejoice in the power of the Holy Spirit.

addressing the congregation

By their promises made before us this day, _____ and _____ have united themselves as husband and wife in sacred covenant. Those whom God has joined together let no one separate.

(B)

Pastor, addressing the congregation

Those whom God has joined together let no one separate.

addressing the couple

_____ and _____, you are wife and husband with the blessing of Christ's church. Be merciful in all your ways, kind in heart, and humble in mind. Accept life, and be most patient and tolerant with one another. Forgive as freely as God has forgiven you. And, above everything else, be truly loving. Let the peace of Christ rule in your hearts, remembering that as members of one body you are called to live in harmony, and never forget to be thankful for what God has done for you.

Blessing

If they are able, the couple may stand or kneel, with children from previous relationships who will share their household, if any, standing nearby. A blessing may be given for the couple or the family.

(A) blessing for the couple

Pastor

The grace of Christ attend you;
the love of God surround you;
the Holy Spirit keep you
that you may grow
in holy love,
find delight in each other always,
and remain faithful
until your life's end.

People

Amen.

(B) blessing for the family

Pastor

May the God
of Sarah and Abraham,
who watches over all the families of the earth,
bless your new family
and establish your home
in peace and steadfast love.

People

Amen.

Passing the Peace

The one presiding may invite those who are able to stand and exchange gestures of peace.

Pastor

The peace of God be with you always.

People

And also with you.

The bride and groom may embrace. Using the same words as the pastor or similar ones, the groom and bride may move among the congregation exchanging the peace. After passing the peace, the people may be seated, and the couple may return to their places.

Prayer of Thanksgiving

The people may be seated. One of these or a similar prayer of thanksgiving and intercession may be offered.

Pastor

Let us pray.

(A)

Pastor

Most gracious God, we give you thanks for your tender love. You sent Jesus Christ to come among us, to be born of a human mother, and to make the way of the cross into the way of life. We thank you, too, for consecrating the union of a man and a woman in Christ's name.

By the power of your Holy Spirit, pour out the abundance of your blessing on _____ and _____. Defend them from every enemy. Lead them into all peace. Let their love for each other be a seal on their hearts, a mantle about their shoulders, and a crown on their heads. Bless them in their work and in their companionship, in their sleeping and in their waking, in their joys and in their sorrows, in their lives and in their deaths. Nurture them in a community of the faithful gathered about you.

(B)

Pastor

Merciful God, we thank you for your love that lives within us and calls us from loneliness to companionship. We thank you for all who have gone before us: for Adam and Eve, for Sarah and Abraham, for Joseph and Mary, and for countless parents whose names we do not know.

We thank you for our own parents, and for all, whether married or single, who are mother or father to us, as we grow to the fullness of the stature of Christ.

Bless _____ and _____, that they may have the grace to live the promises they have made. Defend them from all enemies of their love. Teach them the patience of undeserved forgiveness. Bring them to old age, rejoicing in love's winter more fully than in its springtime.

•

The following words of the prayer may be used if children are present who will share in the couple's household. If these words are not used, continue with option A or B of the prayer.

Pastor

Bless (this child/these children), _____, that (he/she/they) may find in this new home a haven of love and joy where Jesus Christ is honored in kind words and tender deeds.

•

(A)

Pastor

Finally, in your mercy, bring _____ and _____ to that table where your saints feast for ever in your heavenly home; through Jesus Christ our sovereign Savior who, with you and the Holy Spirit, lives and reigns, one God, for ever and ever.

People

Amen.

(B)

Pastor

At the last, receive them and all of us at the love feast prepared for all the faithful in your eternal home, where Jesus Christ, with you and the Holy Spirit, one God, reigns in love for ever.

People

Amen.

Prayer of Our Savior

Standing, sitting, or kneeling, all may sing or say the prayer received from Jesus Christ.

(A)

All

Our Father in heaven, hallowed be your name, your kingdom come, your will be done, on earth as in heaven. Give us today our daily bread. Forgive us our sins as we forgive those who sin against us. Save us from the time of trial and deliver us from evil. For the kingdom, the power, and the glory are yours now and for ever. Amen.

(B)

All

Our Father, who art in heaven, hallowed be thy name. Thy kingdom come. Thy will be done on earth as it is in heaven. Give us this day our daily bread. And forgive us our trespasses, as we forgive those who trespass against us. And lead us not into temptation, but deliver us from evil. For thine is the kingdom, and the power, and the glory, for ever and ever. Amen.

(C)

All

Our Father, who art in heaven, hallowed be thy name. Thy kingdom come. Thy will be done on earth as it is in heaven. Give us this day our daily bread. And forgive us our debts, as we forgive our debtors. And lead us not into temptation, but deliver us from evil. For thine is the kingdom, and the power, and the glory, for ever. Amen.

Benediction

All who are able may stand. One of these or another blessing may be given for all present.

(A)

Pastor

Go forth in the love of God; go forth in hope and joy, knowing that God is with you always.

And the peace of God, which passes all understanding, keep your hearts and minds in the knowledge and love of God and of Christ Jesus; and the blessing of God, Creator, Redeemer, and Sanctifier, be with you, and remain with you always.

People

Amen.

(B)

Pastor

May God bless you and keep you. May God's face shine upon you and be gracious to you. May God look upon you with kindness and give you peace.

People

Amen.

Hymn or Postlude

A hymn may be sung or other suitable music offered as the wedding party and congregation depart.

Source: *Book of Worship, United Church of Christ*. New York: United Church of Christ Office for Church Life and Leadership, 1986. The book contains provisions for celebrating Holy Communion.

The Uniting Church in Australia Wedding Service

THE MARRIAGE SERVICE

The Gathering of the Community

The people stand as the wedding party enters the church.

If a member or friend of the bride's family escorts her into the church, that person brings her to where the bridegroom is standing and then takes a seat in the congregation.

The persons to be married stand together before the minister, the bridegroom standing at the right hand of the bride, in the presence of two appointed witnesses and the congregation.

1 Greeting

The minister says:

Grace to you and peace
from God our Father and the Lord Jesus Christ.
   (Romans 1:7)

Amen.

or

The Lord be with you.
And also with you.

We have come together in the presence of God
to witness the marriage of

_____

and _____,

to surround them with our prayers,
and to share in their joy.

The minister may welcome the people.

2 Scripture Sentences

The minister calls the people to worship with one or more Scripture sentence(s), such as:

Come, let us sing to the Lord;
let us come before his presence with thanksgiving.
   (Psalm 95:1–2)

Give thanks to the Lord, for he is good;
his mercy endures for ever. (Psalm 118:1)

This is the day which the Lord has made;
let us rejoice and be glad in it. (Psalm 118:24)

God is love,
and those who live in love live in God,
and God lives in them. (1 John 4:16)

3 Hymn

A hymn or song may be sung.

4 Declaration of Purpose

The minister says:

Marriage is appointed by God.
The church believes that marriage
is a gift of God in creation

164

and a means of grace in which man and woman
become one in heart, mind, and body.

Marriage is the sacred and life-long union
of a man and a woman
who give themselves to each other in love and trust.
It signifies the mystery of the union
between Christ and the church.

Marriage is given that husband and wife
may enrich and encourage each other
in every part of their life together.

Marriage is given that with delight and tenderness
they may know each other in love,
and through their physical union
may strengthen the union of their lives.

Marriage is given that children may be born
and brought up in security and love,
that home and family life may be strengthened,
and that society may stand upon firm foundations.

Marriage is a way of life which all people should
    honor;
it is not to be entered into lightly or selfishly,
but responsibly and in the love of God.

_____ and _____ are now to
    begin this way of life
which God has created and Christ has blessed.
Therefore, on this their wedding day, we pray for
    them,
asking that they may fulfill God's purpose
for the whole of their lives.

> *The bride and bridegroom and their attendants may
> sit.*

The Service of the Word

5 Scriptural Readings

> *A prayer for illumination may be offered.*

> *One or more passages of Scripture shall be read.*

> *The following may be used after the final reading:*

This is the word of the Lord.
Thanks be to God.

> *A Bible may be presented to the couple here or after the
> sermon.*

> *The minister may say:*

Take this Bible.
May the gospel of Christ inspire you
as you build your home and marriage.

6 Sermon

The Marriage

7 Prayer

> *The minister calls the people to prayer and uses one of
> the following prayers or offers free prayer:*

Gracious God,
your generous love surrounds us,
and everything we enjoy comes from you.
In your great love
you have given us the gift of marriage.
Bless _____ and _____ as they
    pledge their lives to each other;
that their love may continue to grow
and be the true reflection of your love for us all;
through Jesus Christ our Lord.
Amen.

> *or*

Father,
you have made the covenant of marriage a holy
    mystery,
a symbol of Christ's love for the church.
Hear our prayers for _____ and
_____.
With faith in you and in each other,
they pledge their love today.
May their lives always bear witness
to the reality of that love.
We ask this through your Son,
our Lord Jesus Christ.
Amen.

> *or*

Living God,
you are always faithful in your love for us.

Look mercifully upon _____ and

_____

who have come seeking your blessing.
Let the Holy Spirit rest upon them,
so that with steadfast love
they may honor the promises they make this day;
through Jesus Christ our Savior.
Amen.

8 Declaration of Intent

The bride and bridegroom stand.

Then the minister may ask them:

_____ and _____,
do you believe that God has blessed and guided you,
and now calls you into marriage?

The bridegroom and bride each answer:

I do.

The minister shall ask the bridegroom:

_____, will you give yourself to
_____ to be her husband,
to live together in the covenant of marriage?
Will you love her, comfort her,
honor and protect her,
and, forsaking all others, be faithful to her
as long as you both shall live?

He answers:

I will.

The minister shall ask the bride:

_____, will you give yourself to
_____ to be his wife,
to live together in the covenant of marriage?
Will you love him, comfort him,
honor and protect him,
and, forsaking all others, be faithful to him,
as long as you both shall live?

She answers:

I will.

9 Affirmation by the Families

If one of the following questions is used, those answering are asked to stand and may be addressed by name.

Do you, the parents of _____ and

_____,

give your blessing to their marriage?

The parents of the bride and bridegroom say:

We do.

or

Do you, on behalf of your family,
give your blessing to this marriage?

A member of each family says:

I do.

or

Do you, on behalf of both families,
give your blessing to this marriage?

A member of one family says:

I do.

10 Affirmation by the People

The minister may ask the people:

Will you, the families and friends of
_____ and _____,
who have come to share this wedding day,
uphold them in their marriage?

The people say:

We will.

Alternately, the minister may say:

I call upon you, the families and friends of
_____ and _____,
who have come to share this wedding day,
to uphold them in their marriage.

11 The Vows

either **A**

The bride and bridegroom face each other and join hands.

The bridegroom says:

I, _____, in the presence of God,
take you, _____, to be my wife;
to have and to hold
from this day forward,
for better, for worse,
for richer, for poorer,
in sickness and in health,
to love and to cherish,
as long as we both shall live.
This is my solemn vow.

The bride says:

I, _____, in the presence of God,
take you, _____, to be my husband;
to have and to hold
from this day forward,
for better, for worse,
for richer, for poorer,
in sickness and in health,
to love and to cherish,
as long as we both shall live.
This is my solemn vow.

They loose hands.

or **B**

The bride and bridegroom face each other and join hands.

The bridegroom says:

I, _____, take you, _____,
to be my wife,
according to God's holy will.
I will love you,
and share my life with you,
in sickness and in health,
in poverty and in prosperity,
in conflict and in harmony,
as long as we both shall live.
This is my solemn vow.

The bride says:

I, _____, take you, _____,
to be my husband,
according to God's holy will.
I will love you,
and share my life with you,
in sickness and in health,
in poverty and in prosperity,
in conflict and in harmony,
as long as we both shall live.
This is my solemn vow.

They loose hands.

or **C**

The bride and bridegroom face each other and join hands.

The bridegroom says:

I, _____, in the presence of God,
take you, _____, to be my wife.
All that I am I give to you,
and all that I have I share with you.
Whatever the future holds,
I will love you and stand by you,
as long as we both shall live.
This is my solemn vow.

The bride says:

I, _____, in the presence of God,
take you, _____, to be my husband.
All that I am I give to you,
and all that I have I share with you.
Whatever the future holds,
I will love you and stand by you,
as long as we both shall live.
This is my solemn vow.

They loose hands.

or **D**

The bridegroom turns and faces the people, and says:

I ask everyone here to witness
that I, _____, take _____ to be
    my wife,
according to God's holy will.

He then faces the bride, takes her hands, and says:

_____,

all that I am I give to you,
and all that I have I share with you.
Whatever the future holds,
I will love you and stand by you,
as long as we both shall live.
This is my solemn vow.

They loose hands.

The bride turns and faces the people, and says:

I ask everyone here to witness
that I, _____, take _____ to be
   my husband,
according to God's holy will.

She then faces the bridegroom, takes his hands, and says:

_____,

all that I am I give to you,
and all that I have I share with you.
Whatever the future holds,
I will love you and stand by you,
as long as we both shall live.
This is my solemn vow.

They loose hands.

12 Giving of the Rings

The minister receives the ring(s) and may say:

Let us pray:

God of steadfast love,
by your blessing,
let these rings (this ring) be to _____ and

_____

a symbol of the vows
which they have made this day;
through Jesus Christ our Lord.
Amen.

As the giver places the ring on the ring-finger of the other's left hand, the following words may be said:

_____, I give you this ring
as a sign of our marriage
and of the vows which we have made today.

If only one ring is given, the following may be said by the receiver:

_____, I receive this ring
as a sign of our marriage
and of the vows which we have made today.

13 Proclamation of the Marriage

The couple join hands.

The minister asks the people to stand, and addresses them:

Hear the words of our Lord Jesus Christ:
From the beginning of creation,
God made them male and female.
For this reason a man shall leave his father and
   mother
and be joined to his wife,
and the two shall become one.
So they are no longer two but one.
Let no one separate those whom God has joined
   together. (Mark 10:6–9)

Before God and in the presence of us all,
_____ and _____ have made
   their solemn vows.
They have confirmed their marriage
by the joining of hands
and by the giving and receiving of rings (a ring).
In the name of the Father,
and of the Son, and of the Holy Spirit,
I therefore proclaim
that they are now husband and wife.

The Blessing of the Marriage

14 Acclamations

The following may be said by the minister only, or used responsively with the people.

Blessed are you, heavenly Father:
You give joy to the bridegroom and bride.

Blessed are you, Lord Jesus Christ:
You have brought new life to the world.

Blessed are you, Holy Spirit of God:
You bring us together in love.

Blessed be Father, Son, and Holy Spirit:
One God to be praised for ever. Amen.

15 Blessing

The couple may kneel or stand as the minister says one of the following blessings:

God the Father make you holy in his love;
God the Son enrich you with his grace;
God the Holy Spirit strengthen you with joy.
The Lord bless you and keep you in eternal life.
Amen.

or

The riches of God's grace be upon you,
that you may live together in faith and love
and receive the blessings of eternal life.
May almighty God,
who creates you, redeems you, and guides you,
bless you now and always.
Amen.

The couple stand.

16 The Peace

The minister gives the greeting of peace to the couple and to all the people:

The peace of the Lord be always with you.
And also with you.

The minister may give a sign of peace to the husband and the wife.

The minister may say to the couple:

In peace, greet each other with a kiss.

The couple may move to where their parents are standing and greet them.

The people sit.

17 Prayers

The couple may kneel.

The minister or lay person(s) may offer free prayer or may use resources from sections A, B, or C.

either **A**

Some or all of the following petitions may be used.

Each petition or a grouping of petitions may conclude with:

Lord, hear us.
Lord, hear our prayer.

In peace, let us pray to the Lord:

All grace comes from you, O God,
and you alone are the source of eternal life.
Bless your servants _____ and

_____,
that they may faithfully live together
to the end of their lives.

May they be patient and gentle,
ready to trust each other,
and to face together the challenge of the future.

May they pray together in joy and in sorrow,
and always give thanks for the gift of each other.

Be with them in all their happiness;
that your joy may be in them,
and their joy may be full.

Strengthen them in every time of trouble,
that they may bear each other's burdens,
and so fulfill the law of Christ.

Give _____ and _____ grace,
    when they hurt each other,
to recognize and acknowledge their fault,
to ask for each other's forgiveness,
and to know your mercy and love.

May your peace dwell in their home,
and be a sign of hope for peace in the world.

Let their home be a place of welcome,
that its happiness may be freely shared.

Through loving one another in Christ,
may they be strengthened to love Christ in their
    neighbor.

May they be creative in their daily work,
and find fulfilment in the life of their community.

The following petition may be included:

May _____ and _____ enjoy the
   gift and heritage of children.
Grant that they may be loving and wise parents,
with grace to bring up their children
to know you, to love you, and to serve you.

The following petition may be included if there are children/grandchildren of a previous marriage:

May _____ and _____ enjoy the
   gift and heritage of their children.
Grant them the grace to share their love (and faith)
with _____ and _____ (*names of
   children*)
that they may grow together as a loving family.

Bless the parents and families of _____
   and _____,
that they may be united in love and friendship.

Grant that all married people
who have witnessed these vows today
may find their lives strengthened
and their loyalties confirmed.

We ask these prayers in the name of Christ our Lord.
Amen.

or **B**

A selection of the following prayers may be used.

Let us pray for _____ and _____
   in their life together:

either

Most gracious God,
we bless you for your tender love
in sending Jesus Christ to come among us,
born of a human mother.
We give you thanks that he grew up
in a home in Nazareth,
and joined in the celebration of a marriage
in Cana of Galilee.
By the power of the Holy Spirit,
give your blessing to _____ and
   _____.

Let their love for each other
be a seal upon their hearts,
a mantle about their shoulders,

and a crown upon their heads.
Bless them in their work and in their companionship,
in their joys and in their sorrows.
And finally in your mercy
bring them to your heavenly home;
through Jesus Christ our Lord.
Amen.

or

Faithful Lord, source of all love,
pour down your grace upon _____ and
_____,
that they may fulfil the vows they have made today,
and reflect your steadfast love
in their life-long faithfulness to each other.
Help us to support them in their life together.
Give them courage and patience,
affection and understanding,
and love toward you,
toward each other,
and toward the world;
that they may continue to grow
in Jesus Christ our Lord.
Amen.

or

Creator God, giver of life,
bless _____ and _____ whom
   you have joined in marriage.
Grant them wisdom and devotion in their life together,
that each may be for the other a strength in need,
a comfort in sorrow, and a companion in joy.
So unite their wills in your will,
and their spirits in your Spirit,
that they may live and grow together in love and
   peace
all the days of their life;
through Jesus Christ our Lord.
Amen.

Let us pray for _____ and _____'s
   families:

Gracious God,
you have called us to live in loving families,

and by your generous love
all the families on earth are blessed.
We pray today for the parents and families of
_____ and _____.
We recall the gracious influences and loving deeds
that have surrounded _____ and
_____ in their homes.
And for their parents we ask continuing health,
fulfilment of life,
and the joy of knowing their children's children;
through Jesus Christ our Lord.
Amen.

Let us pray for all families:

Gracious Father,
you bless family life and renew your people.
Enrich husbands and wives, parents and children
more and more with your grace,
that, strengthening and supporting each other,
they may serve those in need
and be a sign of the fulfilment of your kingdom,
where, with your Son Jesus Christ and the Holy
    Spirit,
you live and reign,
one God through all ages.
Amen.

or **C**

Eternal God,
without your grace no promise is sure.
Strengthen _____ and _____
with patience, kindness, gentleness,
and all other gifts of the Holy Spirit,
so that they may fulfil the vows they have made.
Keep them faithful to each other and to you.
Fill them with such love and joy
that they may build a home of peace and welcome.
Guide them by your word to serve you all their days.
Enable us all, O God,
to do your will in each of our homes and lives.
Enrich us with your grace,
so that, encouraging and supporting one another,
we may serve those in need
and hasten the coming
of peace, love, and justice on earth;
through Jesus Christ our Lord.
Amen.

18 The Lord's Prayer

*The minister or lay person concludes the prayers by
saying:*

And now let us pray together
in the words our Savior gave us:

either

Our Father in heaven,
    hallowed be your name,
    your kingdom come,
    your will be done,
        on earth as in heaven.
Give us today our daily bread.
Forgive us our sins,
    as we forgive those who sin against us.
Save us from the time of trial
    and deliver us from evil.

For the kingdom, the power, and the glory are yours
    now and for ever. Amen.

or

Our Father, who art in heaven,
    hallowed be thy name,
    thy kingdom come,
    thy will be done
        on earth as it is in heaven.
Give us this day our daily bread.
And forgive us our trespasses,
    as we forgive those who trespass against us.
And lead us not into temptation,
    but deliver us from evil.

For thine is the kingdom, the power, and the glory,
    for ever and ever. Amen.

19 Holy Communion

*If Holy Communion is to be celebrated, see section 19
below and note 1 at the end of this order.*

20 Hymn

A hymn or song may be sung.

*At the conclusion, the people remain standing for the
Blessing.*

21 Blessing

The blessing of God almighty,
the Father, the Son, and the Holy Spirit,
be upon you and remain with you always.
Amen.

22 Signing of the Marriage Certificates

•

19 Holy Communion

A communion hymn may be sung.

The service of holy communion begins at The Setting of the Table. The newly married couple may bring gifts of bread and wine to the Lord's table.

The following form of the Great Prayer of Thanksgiving may be used at a marriage:

The Lord be with you.
And also with you.

Lift up your hearts.
We lift them to the Lord.

Let us give thanks to the Lord our God.
It is right to give our thanks and praise.

Loving God,
on this joyous occasion
we delight to give you thanks.
You made us in your image,
creating us male and female.
With Abraham and Sarah you made a covenant
that through them all people might be blessed.
To Mary and Joseph you gave a Son
who has wedded all people to yourself.
You have given us the gift of marriage
that we may fulfil one another in love.

And so we praise you
with the faithful of every time and place,
joining with choirs of angels and the whole creation
in the eternal hymn:

**Holy, holy, holy Lord, God of power and might,
heaven and earth are full of your glory.
Hosanna in the highest.**

**Blessed is he who comes in the name of the
Lord.
Hosanna in the highest.**

We bless you that you loved the world so much
that you gave your only Son Jesus Christ to be our
Savior.
He suffered and died for the sin of the world.
You raised him from the dead
that we too might have new life.
He ascended to be with you in glory,
and by the Holy Spirit he is with us always.
He loved the church and gave himself for it,
giving us an example for the love of husband and
wife.

On the night before he died,
Jesus took bread,
and when he had given you thanks
he broke it, and gave it to his disciples saying:
Take, eat. This is my body which is given for you.
Do this in remembrance of me.

After supper, he took the cup,
and again giving you thanks
he gave it to his disciples, saying:
Drink from this, all of you.
This is my blood of the new covenant
which is shed for you and for many
for the forgiveness of sins.
Do this, as often as you drink it, in remembrance of
me.

Therefore,
in remembrance of all your mighty acts in Jesus
Christ
we ask you to accept
this sacrifice of praise and thanksgiving,
which we offer in union with Christ's sacrifice.

Send the Holy Spirit upon us and what we do here;
that we and these gifts, touched by your Spirit,
may be signs of life and love to each other
and to all the world.

Through Christ, with Christ, in Christ,
in the unity of the Holy Spirit,
all glory is yours, eternal Father,
now and for ever. **Amen.**

Note 1. If both the bridegroom and bride are regular communicants, they may desire the inclusion of holy communion in their wedding service. Because holy communion is the celebration of the community of faith, it should be open to all people present who would normally communicate.

Source: *Uniting in Worship Leader's Book*. Prepared by the Assembly Commission on Liturgy and approved by the Assembly Standing Committee for use in the Uniting Church in Australia. Melbourne: Uniting Church Press, 1988.

Part III

Additional Helps

Scriptures for the Wedding Service

Old Testament Readings

Genesis 1:26–31
Genesis 2:4–9, 15–24
Genesis 2:18–24

Ruth 1:16–17

Proverbs 3:3–6

Ecclesiastes 26:1–4

Song of Solomon 2:10–13
Song of Solomon 8:6–7

Isaiah 54:5–8
Isaiah 63:7–9

Jeremiah 31:31–34

Hosea 2:16–23

Selections from the Psalms

8
22:25–31
23
33
34
37:3–7
67
95:1–7
100
103:1–5, 15–18
112
117
121
127
128
136
136:1–9, 26
145
148
150

New Testament Readings

Matthew 5:1–10
Matthew 5:13–16
Matthew 7:21, 24–29
Matthew 19:3–6
Matthew 22:35–40

Mark 10:6–9, 13–16

Luke 6:36–38

John 2:1–11
John 15:1–17

Romans 8:31–39
Romans 12:1–2, 9–18

1 Corinthians 6:15–20
1 Corinthians 12:31–13:13

Ephesians 3:14–21
Ephesians 5:1–2, 21–33

Colossians 3:12–17

1 Peter 3:1–9

1 John 4:7–16

Revelation 19:1, 5–9

Sample "A" Worksheet

WEDDING SERVICE
for

GROOM'S FULL NAME:

David Edward Franklin

How would you like to be addressed in the wedding service (i.e., Jonathan, John, John William, etc.)?

David

Date of the wedding: *4-25-91*

Time: *5:00 PM*

BRIDE'S FULL NAME:

Meredith Anne Armstrong

How would you like to be addressed in the wedding service (i.e., Catherine, Emily Catherine, Cathy, etc.)?

Meredith

Date of the rehearsal: *4-24-91*

Time: *7:30 PM*

Place of the wedding: *First Presbyterian Church*

Below, write in the selection letter you have chosen for each category. For instance, if you have chosen Selection D under Category 1, then fill in the blank with that letter in Category 1. A complete wedding service based on this worksheet directly follows.

☑ **CATEGORY 1: OPENING STATEMENT**

Selection __*B*__

☑ **CATEGORY 2: ADDRESS TO THE COUPLE AND/OR SCRIPTURE READING(S)**

(This category is optional. Some opening statements already contain words that address the couple, and redundancy is possible. A scripture reading or readings may be selected; if you wish to use one or more scripture readings here, write "O" in the blank below. A list of suggested scripture readings is given on p. 177.)

Selection __*B*__

(If you choose Selection O, list your scripture text[s] here.)

Scripture text(s) _____

_____

_____

☑ **CATEGORY 3: OPENING PRAYER**

Selection __*I*__

☑ **CATEGORY 4: QUESTIONS OF INTENT**

Selection __*J*__

☑ **CATEGORY 5: LEAVETAKING**

(This section is optional and may be omitted. You can choose a selection, omit the category, or, in consultation with the minister, write your own response.)

Selection __*H*__

We suggest this response:

_____

We choose to omit this section [ ]

☑ **CATEGORY 6: THE VOWS**

Selection __*M*__

☑ **CATEGORY 7: EXCHANGE OF RINGS**

Selection __*Q*__

☑ **CATEGORY 8: DECLARATION OF MARRIAGE**

Selection __*G*__

☑ **CATEGORY 9: PRAYER FOR THE MARRIAGE**

(You may wish to include more than one prayer. If this is your desire, fill in more than one blank.)

Selection ___D___ _____ _____

☑ **CATEGORY 10: THE LORD'S PRAYER**

(It is wise to choose the rendition of the Lord's Prayer that is most familiar to the worshiping congregation that will be in attendance at your wedding. Consult your minister if you are unsure about this. Or, you may have the Lord's Prayer sung by a soloist.)

Selection _____

The Lord's Prayer will be sung [X]

Soloist's name: ___Ellen J. Brown___

❑ **CATEGORY 10A: SPECIAL MUSIC**

(Special music may be inserted here. If you plan to have special music as part of your service, indicate the title of the piece and the one singing or playing. In most cases, you would not want special music in this location if the Lord's Prayer is being sung.)

Special music title(s):

_____

_____

Performed by: _____

☑ **CATEGORY 11: BENEDICTION**

Selection ___M___

Special Music Note

In addition to Category 10a, there are other places in the wedding service where special music may be appropriate. One such place is after Category 4 (or 5), just prior to the vows. It is also traditional in some congregations to sing hymns during the wedding, and this is ordinarily done at the beginning of the service. However, you may wish to have music in another place in the service. If you desire to have other special music within the service, or to have congregational hymns, please indicate your wish here:

We would like to have additional special music after category _____

Title: _____

Performed by: _____

We would like to include a congregational hymn(s) after category _____

Hymn title(s): _____

_____

Are there other suggestions, concerns, or questions you have about your wedding service? If so, please indicate them in the following space:

_____

_____

_____

_____

_____

_____

_____

After you complete this worksheet, you will need to go through it with your minister. He or she may have other suggestions that will enhance the meaning and beauty of your service. After the minister has approved the service,

you may need to make arrangements to have the wedding service typed. Normally, the church secretary will be able to type it and have it ready before the rehearsal date. Confer with the minister or church secretary about this.

Sample "A" Wedding Service Using the Completed Sample "A" Worksheet

WEDDING SERVICE
for
DAVID EDWARD FRANKLIN
and
MEREDITH ANNE ARMSTRONG

April 25, 1991
5:00 PM
First Presbyterian Church

I

The persons to be married stand before the minster with the man to the right of the woman. The minister shall say:

Friends, we are gathered together here in the presence of God and in the fellowship of this Christian community to join together Meredith and David in Christian marriage. Christian marriage is a covenant of faith and trust between a man and woman, established within their shared commitment in the covenant of faith in Jesus Christ as Lord. Therefore, it requires of both man and woman:

openness of life and thought
  freedom from doubt and suspicion,
    and
      commitment to speak the truth in love
        as they grow into Christ
          who is the head of the church.

Christian marriage, furthermore, is a covenant of hope that endures all things and in which both husband and wife commit themselves to interpret each other's behavior with understanding and compassion, never giving up trying to communicate with each other.

Christian marriage, therefore, is a covenant of love in which both husband and wife empty themselves of their own concerns and take upon themselves the concerns of each other in loving each other as Christ loved the church and gave himself for it.

Therefore, this covenant is not to be entered into unadvisedly or lightly, but reverently, discreetly, advisedly, and in awe of God.

Into this holy union these two persons come now to be joined.

II

The minister addresses the couple saying:

I encourage you both to remember that:

Love is patient and kind;
love is not jealous or boastful;
it is not arrogant or rude.
Love does not insist on its own way;
it is not irritable or resentful;

180

it does not rejoice at wrong,
but rejoices in the right.

Love bears all things,
believes all things,
hopes all things,
endures all things.
(1 Corinthians 13:4–7, RSV)

III

The minister says:

Let us pray.

Eternal God, as you gladdened the wedding at Cana in Galilee by the presence of your Son, Jesus, so by his presence now make the occasion of this wedding one of rejoicing. In your favor look upon Meredith and David, about to be joined in marriage, and grant that they might enjoy love and happiness in their relationship, as they look to serve each other and you. Amen.

IV

The minister shall say to the man:

David, will you have this woman to be your wife, and be faithful to her alone?

The man shall answer:

I will, with the help of God.

The minister shall say to the woman:

Meredith, will you have this man to be your husband, and be faithful to him alone?

The woman will answer:

I will, with the help of God.

V

The minister may address the families of the bride and groom:

Members of the Franklin and Armstrong families, do you give your blessing to Meredith and David, and promise to do everything in your power to uphold them in their marriage?

Answer:

We give our blessing
and promise our loving support.

The families may be seated.

VI

The bride and groom join hands and face each other. The man says:

I, David, take you, Meredith, to be my wedded wife; and I do promise and covenant to be your loving and faithful husband; for better, for worse; for richer, for poorer; in sickness and in health; so long as we both shall live.

The woman says:

I, Meredith, take you, David, to be my wedded husband; and I do promise and covenant to be your loving and faithful wife; for better, for worse; for richer, for poorer; in sickness and in health; so long as we both shall live.

VII

The minister may ask God's blessing on the rings as follows:

Bless, O Lord, these rings to be a sign of the vows by which this man and this woman have bound themselves to each other; through Jesus Christ our Lord. Amen.

The man places the ring on the ring finger of the other's hand and says:

Meredith, I give you this ring as a symbol of my vow, and with all that I am, and all that I have, I honor you, in the Name of God.

The woman places the ring on the ring finger of the other's hand and says:

David, I give you this ring as a symbol of my vow, and with all that I am, and all that I have, I honor you, in the Name of God.

VIII

Then shall the minister join their hands together and, with his hand on their united hands, shall say:

Forasmuch as Meredith and David have consented together in holy wedlock, and have witnessed the same before God and this company, and thereto have pledged their faith each to the other and have declared the same by joining hands and by giving and receiving rings; I pronounce that they are husband and wife together, in the name of the Father, and of the Son, and of the Holy Spirit. Those whom God has joined together let no one put asunder. Amen.

IX

The couple may kneel.

Let us pray.

Eternal God,
without your grace no promise is sure.

Strengthen David and Meredith with patience, kindness, gentleness, and all other gifts of your Spirit,
so that they may fulfill the vows they have made.
Keep them faithful to each other and to you.
Fill them with such love and joy
that they may build a home of peace and welcome.
Guide them by your word
to serve you all their days.

Enable us all, O God,
in each of our homes and lives to do your will.
Enrich us with your grace
so that, encouraging and supporting one another,
we may serve those in need
and may hasten the coming of peace, love, and justice on earth,
through Jesus Christ our Lord.

Amen.

X

The Lord's Prayer sung by Ellen J. Brown.

XI

Almighty God, Father, Son, and Holy Spirit, keep you in his light and truth and love now and forever. Amen.

Sample "B" Worksheet

WEDDING SERVICE
for

GROOM'S FULL NAME:

Tyler Scott Williamson

How would you like to be addressed in the wedding service (i.e., Jonathan, John, John William, etc.)?

Tyler

Date of the wedding: *9-13-91*
Time: *3 PM*

BRIDE'S FULL NAME:

Emily Elizabeth Crisp

How would you like to be addressed in the wedding service (i.e., Catherine, Emily Catherine, Cathy, etc.)?

Emily

Date of the rehearsal: *9-12-91*
Time: *6 PM*

Place of the wedding: *St. Stephens Church*

Below, write in the selection letter you have chosen for each category. For instance, if you have chosen Selection D under Category 1, then fill in the blank with that letter in Category 1. A complete wedding service based on this worksheet directly follows.

☑ **CATEGORY 1: OPENING STATEMENT**

Selection *D*

☑ **CATEGORY 2: ADDRESS TO THE COUPLE AND/OR SCRIPTURE READING(S)**

(This category is optional. Some opening statements already contain words that address the couple, and redundancy is possible. A scripture reading or readings may be selected; if you wish to use one or more scripture readings here, write "O" in the blank below. A list of suggested scripture readings is given on p. 177.)

Selection *O*

(If you choose Selection O, list your scripture text[s] here.)

Scripture text(s) *1 John 4:7–12*

☑ **CATEGORY 3: OPENING PRAYER**

Selection *J*

☑ **CATEGORY 4: QUESTIONS OF INTENT**

Selection *Q*

☑ **CATEGORY 5: LEAVETAKING**

(This section is optional and may be omitted. You can choose a selection, omit the category, or, in consultation with the minister, write your own response.)

Selection *V*

We suggest this response:

We choose to omit this section [ ]

☑ **CATEGORY 6: THE VOWS**

Selection *W*

☑ **CATEGORY 7: EXCHANGE OF RINGS**

Selection *A*

☑ **CATEGORY 8: DECLARATION OF MARRIAGE**

Selection *C*

☑ CATEGORY 9: PRAYER FOR THE MARRIAGE

(You may wish to include more than one prayer. If this is your desire, fill in more than one blank.)

Selection _____V_____ _____ _____

☑ CATEGORY 10: THE LORD'S PRAYER

(It is wise to choose the rendition of the Lord's Prayer that is most familiar to the worshiping congregation that will be in attendance at your wedding. Consult your minister if you are unsure about this. Or, you may have the Lord's Prayer sung by a soloist.)

Selection _____A_____

The Lord's Prayer will be sung [ ]

Soloist's name: _____

☐ CATEGORY 10A: SPECIAL MUSIC

(Special music may be inserted here. If you plan to have special music as part of your service, indicate the title of the piece and the one singing or playing. In most cases, you would not want special music in this location if the Lord's Prayer is being sung.)

Special music title(s):

_____

_____

Performed by: _____

☑ CATEGORY 11: BENEDICTION

Selection _____U_____

Special Music Note

In addition to Category 10a, there are other places in the wedding service where special music may be appropriate. One such place is after Category 4 (or 5), just prior to the vows. It is also traditional in some congregations to sing hymns during the wedding, and this is ordinarily done at the beginning of the service. However, you may wish to have music in another place in the service. If you desire to have other special music within the service, or to have congregational hymns, please indicate your wish here:

We would like to have additional special music after category _____4_____

Title: _____My Heart Ever Faithful_____

Performed by: _____L. Kittrell_____

We would like to include a congregational hymn(s) after category _____

Hymn title(s): _____

_____

Are there other suggestions, concerns, or questions you have about your wedding service? If so, please indicate them in the following space:

_____

_____

_____

_____

_____

_____

After you complete this worksheet, you will need to go through it with your minister. He or she may have other suggestions that will enhance the meaning and beauty of your service. After the minister has approved the service, *you may need to make arrangements to have the wedding service typed. Normally, the church secretary will be able to type it and have it ready before the rehearsal date. Confer with the minister or church secretary about this.*

Sample "B" Wedding Service Using the Completed Sample "B" Worksheet

---

**WEDDING SERVICE
for
TYLER SCOTT WILLIAMSON
and
EMILY ELIZABETH CRISP**

**September 13, 1991
3:00 PM
St. Stephens Church**

I

The persons to be married stand before the minister with the man to the right of the woman. The minister shall say:

Grace to you and peace
from God our Father and the Lord Jesus Christ.
(Romans 1:7)

or

Minister:

The Lord be with you.

People:

And also with you.

We have come together in the presence of God
to witness the marriage of

Tyler Scott Williamson
and Emily Elizabeth Crisp,
to surround them with our prayers,
and to share in their joy.

The minister calls the people to worship with one or more scriptural sentences, such as:

Come, let us sing to the Lord;
let us come before his presence with thanksgiving.
(Psalm 95:1–2)

Give thanks to the Lord, for he is good;
his mercy endures for ever. (Psalm 118:1)

This is the day which the Lord has made;
let us rejoice and be glad in it. (Psalm 118:24)

God is love,
and those who live in love live in God,
and God lives in them. (1 John 4:16)

The minister says:

Marriage is appointed by God.
The church believes that marriage
is a gift of God in creation
and a means of grace in which man and woman
become one in heart, mind, and body.

Marriage is the sacred and life-long union
of a man and a woman
who give themselves to each other in love and trust.

185

It signifies the mystery of the union
between Christ and the church.

Marriage is given that husband and wife
may enrich and encourage each other
in every part of their life together.

Marriage is given that with delight and tenderness
they may know each other in love,
and through their physical union
may strengthen the union of their lives.

Marriage is given that children may be born
and brought up in security and love,
that home and family life may be strengthened,
and that society may stand upon firm foundations.

Marriage is a way of life which all people should
     honor;
it is not to be entered into lightly or selfishly,
but responsibly and in the love of God.

Emily and Tyler are now to begin this way of life
which God has created and Christ has blessed.
Therefore, on this their wedding day, we pray for
     them,
asking that they may fulfill God's purpose
for the whole of their lives.

II

Beloved, let us love one another; for love is of God, and he who loves is born of God and knows God. He who does not love does not know God; for God is love. In this the love of God was made manifest among us, that God sent his only Son into the world, so that we might live through him. In this is love, not that we loved God but that he loved us and sent his Son to be the expiation for our sins. Beloved, if God so loved us, we also ought to love one another. No man has ever seen God; if we love one another, God abides in us and his love is perfected in us. (1 John 4:7–12, RSV)

III

Let us pray.

Gracious God, always faithful in your love for us, we rejoice in your presence. You create love. You unite us in one human family. You offer your word and lead us in light. You open your loving arms and embrace us with strength. May the presence of Christ fill our hearts with new joy and make new the lives of your servants whose marriage we celebrate. Bless all creation through this sign of your love shown in the love of Tyler and Emily for each other. May the power of your Holy Spirit sustain them and all of us in love that knows no end.
Amen.

IV

The persons to be married shall stand with their attendants before the minister, who shall ask the man:

Tyler, will you receive Emily as your wife and bind yourself to her in the covenant of marriage? Will you promise to love and honor her in true devotion; to rejoice with her in time of felicity and grieve with her in times of sorrow; and be faithful to her as long as you both shall live?

Man:

I will, with the help of God.

The minister shall ask the woman:

Emily, will you receive Tyler as your husband and bind yourself to him in the covenant of marriage? Will you promise to love and honor him in true devotion; to rejoice with him in times of felicity and grieve with him in times of sorrow; and be faithful to him as long as you both shall live?

Woman:

I will, with the help of God.

IVa

Special Music:
"My Heart Ever Faithful" (Bach/Schirmer)
Sung by Laney Kittrell, soloist
Accompanied by Kathryn M. Butler

V

Do you the families of Emily and Tyler promise to pray for and support this new relationship which they enter as husband and wife?

A representative of each family (i.e., best man or father and presenter of the bride or maid/matron of honor) shall answer:

We do.

VI

The woman and man face each other, joining hands. The man says:

In the name of God,
I, Tyler, take you, Emily,
to be my wife,
to have and to hold
from this day forward,
for better for worse,
for richer for poorer,
in sickness and in health,
to love and to cherish,
until we are parted by death.
This is my solemn vow.

The woman says:

In the name of God,
I, Emily, take you, Tyler,
to be my husband,
to have and to hold
from this day forward,
for better for worse,
for richer for poorer,
in sickness and in health,
to love and to cherish,

until we are parted by death.
This is my solemn vow.

VII

The minister says:

What token do you give of this your marriage vow?

The man, placing the ring on the woman's hand, shall say:

This ring I give in token of the covenant made this day between us; in the name of the Father and of the Son and of the Holy Spirit. Amen.

The woman, placing the ring on the man's hand, shall say:

This ring I give in token of the covenant made this day between us; in the name of the Father and of the Son and of the Holy Spirit. Amen.

VIII

The minister addresses the congregation:

Before God
and in the presence of this congregation,
Tyler and Emily have made their solemn vows to
    each other.
They have confirmed their promises by joining of
    hands
[and by the giving and receiving of rings].
Therefore, I proclaim that they are now husband and
    wife.

Blessed be the Father and the Son and the Holy
    Spirit now and forever.

The minister joins the couple's right hands.

The congregation may join the minister saying:

Those whom God has joined together
let no one separate.

The minister addresses the couple:

As God's own,
clothe yourselves with compassion,
kindness, and patience,

forgiving each other
as the Lord has forgiven you,
and crown all these things with love,
which binds everything together in perfect harmony.

(Col. 3:12–14)

IX

Couple may kneel.

Let us pray.

Faithful Lord, source of all love,
pour down your grace upon Emily and Tyler,
that they may fulfill the vows they have made today,
and reflect your steadfast love
in their lifelong faithfulness to each other.
Help us to support them in their life together.
Give them courage and patience,
affection and understanding,
and love toward you,
toward each other,
and toward the world;
that they may continue to grow
in Jesus Christ our Lord.
Amen.

X

Let us pray the prayer our Lord taught us saying:

Our Father, who art in heaven, hallowed be thy name. Thy kingdom come. Thy will be done on earth as it is in heaven. Give us this day our daily bread. And forgive us our debts, as we forgive our debtors. And lead us not into temptation, but deliver us from evil; for thine is the kingdom, and the power, and the glory, forever. Amen.

XI

Go forth in the love of God; go forth in hope and joy, knowing that God is with you always.

And the peace of God, which passes all understanding, keep your hearts and minds in the knowledge and love of God and of Christ Jesus; and the blessing of god, Creator, Redeemer, and Sanctifier, be with you, and remain with you always. Amen.

Wedding Sourcebook Worksheet

═══

WEDDING SERVICE
for

GROOM'S FULL NAME:

_____

How would you like to be addressed in the wedding service (i.e., Jonathan, John, John William, etc.)?

_____

Date of the wedding: _____

Time: _____

BRIDE'S FULL NAME:

_____

How would you like to be addressed in the wedding service (i.e., Catherine, Emily Catherine, Cathy, etc.)?

_____

Date of the rehearsal: _____

Time: _____

Place of the wedding: _____

Below, write in the selection letter you have chosen for each category. For instance, if you have chosen Selection D under Category 1, then fill in the blank with that letter in Category 1. Completed samples of this worksheet can be found in the back of the book (see pp. 178–179, 183–184).

❑ **CATEGORY 1: OPENING STATEMENT**

Selection _____

❑ **CATEGORY 2: ADDRESS TO THE COUPLE AND/OR SCRIPTURE READING(S)**

(This category is optional. Some opening statements already contain words that address the couple, and redundancy is possible. A scripture reading or readings may be selected; if you wish to use one or more scripture readings here, write "O" in the blank below. A list of suggested scripture readings is given on p. 177.)

Selection _____

(If you choose Selection O, list your scripture text[s] here.)

Scripture text(s) _____

_____

_____

❑ **CATEGORY 3: OPENING PRAYER**

Selection _____

❑ **CATEGORY 4: QUESTIONS OF INTENT**

Selection _____

❑ **CATEGORY 5: LEAVETAKING**

(This section is optional and may be omitted. You can choose a selection, omit the category, or, in consultation with the minister, write your own response.)

Selection _____

We suggest this response:

_____

We choose to omit this section [ ]

❑ **CATEGORY 6: THE VOWS**

Selection _____

❑ **CATEGORY 7: EXCHANGE OF RINGS**

Selection _____

❑ **CATEGORY 8: DECLARATION OF MARRIAGE**

Selection _____

❏ **CATEGORY 9: PRAYER FOR THE MARRIAGE**

(You may wish to include more than one prayer. If this is your desire, fill in more than one blank.)

Selection ———— ———— ————

❏ **CATEGORY 10: THE LORD'S PRAYER**

(It is wise to choose the rendition of the Lord's Prayer that is most familiar to the worshiping congregation that will be in attendance at your wedding. Consult your minister if you are unsure about this. Or, you may have the Lord's Prayer sung by a soloist.)

Selection ————

The Lord's Prayer will be sung [   ]

Soloist's name: ———————————————————

❏ **CATEGORY 10A: SPECIAL MUSIC**

(Special music may be inserted here. If you plan to have special music as part of your service, indicate the title of the piece and the one singing or playing. In most cases, you would not want special music in this location if the Lord's Prayer is being sung.)

Special music title(s):

————————————————————————

————————————————————————

Performed by: ——————————————————

❏ **CATEGORY 11: BENEDICTION**

Selection ————

Special Music Note

In addition to Category 10a, there are other places in the wedding service where special music may be appropriate. One such place is after Category 4 (or 5), just prior to the vows. It is also traditional in some congregations to sing hymns during the wedding, and this is ordinarily done at the beginning of the service. However, you may wish to have music in another place in the service. If you desire to have other special music within the service, or to have congregational hymns, please indicate your wish here:

We would like to have additional special music after category ————

Title: ——————————————————————

Performed by: ——————————————————

We would like to include a congregational hymn(s) after category ————

Hymn title(s): —————————————————

————————————————————————

Are there other suggestions, concerns, or questions you have about your wedding service? If so, please indicate them in the following space:

————————————————————————————

————————————————————————————

————————————————————————————

————————————————————————————

————————————————————————————

————————————————————————————

After you complete this worksheet, you will need to go through it with your minister. He or she may have other suggestions that will enhance the meaning and beauty of your service. After the minister has approved the service,

you may need to make arrangements to have the wedding service typed. Normally, the church secretary will be able to type it and have it ready before the rehearsal date. Confer with the minister or church secretary about this.

8468

Wedding Sourcebook Worksheet

WEDDING SERVICE
for

GROOM'S FULL NAME:

_____

How would you like to be addressed in the wedding service (i.e., Jonathan, John, John William, etc.)?

_____

Date of the wedding: _____

Time: _____

BRIDE'S FULL NAME:

_____

How would you like to be addressed in the wedding service (i.e., Catherine, Emily Catherine, Cathy, etc.)?

_____

Date of the rehearsal: _____

Time: _____

Place of the wedding: _____

Below, write in the selection letter you have chosen for each category. For instance, if you have chosen Selection D under Category 1, then fill in the blank with that letter in Category 1. Completed samples of this worksheet can be found in the back of the book (see pp. 178–179, 183–184).

❏ **CATEGORY 1: OPENING STATEMENT**

  Selection _____

❏ **CATEGORY 2: ADDRESS TO THE COUPLE AND/OR SCRIPTURE READING(S)**

(This category is optional. Some opening statements already contain words that address the couple, and redundancy is possible. A scripture reading or readings may be selected; if you wish to use one or more scripture readings here, write "O" in the blank below. A list of suggested scripture readings is given on p. 177.)

  Selection _____

(If you choose Selection O, list your scripture text[s] here.)

Scripture text(s) _____

  _____

  _____

❏ **CATEGORY 3: OPENING PRAYER**

  Selection _____

❏ **CATEGORY 4: QUESTIONS OF INTENT**

  Selection _____

❏ **CATEGORY 5: LEAVETAKING**

(This section is optional and may be omitted. You can choose a selection, omit the category, or, in consultation with the minister, write your own response.)

  Selection _____

We suggest this response:

_____

We choose to omit this section [ ]

❏ **CATEGORY 6: THE VOWS**

  Selection _____

❏ **CATEGORY 7: EXCHANGE OF RINGS**

  Selection _____

❏ **CATEGORY 8: DECLARATION OF MARRIAGE**

  Selection _____

☐ CATEGORY 9: PRAYER FOR THE MARRIAGE

(You may wish to include more than one prayer. If this is your desire, fill in more than one blank.)

Selection _____ _____ _____

☐ CATEGORY 10: THE LORD'S PRAYER

(It is wise to choose the rendition of the Lord's Prayer that is most familiar to the worshiping congregation that will be in attendance at your wedding. Consult your minister if you are unsure about this. Or, you may have the Lord's Prayer sung by a soloist.)

Selection _____

The Lord's Prayer will be sung [   ]

Soloist's name: _____

☐ CATEGORY 10A: SPECIAL MUSIC

(Special music may be inserted here. If you plan to have special music as part of your service, indicate the title of the piece and the one singing or playing. In most cases, you would not want special music in this location if the Lord's Prayer is being sung.)

Special music title(s):

_____

_____

Performed by: _____

☐ CATEGORY 11: BENEDICTION

Selection _____

Special Music Note

In addition to Category 10a, there are other places in the wedding service where special music may be appropriate. One such place is after Category 4 (or 5), just prior to the vows. It is also traditional in some congregations to sing hymns during the wedding, and this is ordinarily done at the beginning of the service. However, you may wish to have music in another place in the service. If you desire to have other special music within the service, or to have congregational hymns, please indicate your wish here:

We would like to have additional special music after category _____

Title: _____

Performed by: _____

We would like to include a congregational hymn(s) after category _____

Hymn title(s): _____

_____

Are there other suggestions, concerns, or questions you have about your wedding service? If so, please indicate them in the following space:

_____

_____

_____

_____

_____

_____

After you complete this worksheet, you will need to go through it with your minister. He or she may have other suggestions that will enhance the meaning and beauty of your service. After the minister has approved the service, *you may need to make arrangements to have the wedding service typed. Normally, the church secretary will be able to type it and have it ready before the rehearsal date. Confer with the minister or church secretary about this.*